Struck from Behind

Struck from Behind

My Memories of God

JAMES C. HOWELL

CASCADE *Books* · Eugene, Oregon

Cascade Books
An Imprint of Wipf and Stock Publishers
199 W. 8th Ave., Suite 3
Eugene, OR 97401

www.wipfandstock.com

ISBN 13: 978-1-61097-932-0

Cataloging-in-Publication data:

Howell, James C.

Struck from behind : my memories of God / James C. Howell.

x + 160 p. ; 23 cm.

ISBN 13: 978-1-61097-932-0

1. Methodist Church—Clergy—Biography. 2. Clergy—United States—Biography. I. Title.

BX 9225 H315 A4 2012

Manufactured in the U.S.A.

Contents

Introduction

WHEN HE WAS JUST twenty years old, Henry David Thoreau jotted down a brief insight in his journal: "Truth strikes us from behind, and in the dark."[1] When I was twenty, I tried never to look over my shoulder. I was hurrying toward my life; the past was past. God was still a newcomer to my little world. My plan was to begin to learn what I could about God, and try to develop a relationship of some substance—and I assumed God was out there in front of me, waiting to be player in my personal drama.

What had not dawned on me then, what had not yet "struck" me, was that God was back there, maybe in the shadows, lurking around, and active all along. When I have remembered moments and people and places from my childhood, adolescence, and even my adult life, I've come to acknowledge over and over what Jacob realized when he woke up in Bethel after sleeping on the ground with a stone for a pillow: "Surely the Lord was in this place, but I did not know it" (Gen 28:16).

I never thought I would write a memoir. I've never been an avid reader of autobiography. So many memoirs seem too self-obsessed, with too much self-analysis. Some memoirs I've read were wonderfully written—but I found myself envying the style more than relishing the story line. My own life story has been one even I would regard as too chaotic, and much of the time even too dull, to be published. I nodded with sympathy when I read a scene in Paul Harding's quirky novel, *Tinkers*: an aging man, thinking to preserve his life story for posterity, borrowed a tape recorder, talked for a while, then rewound so he could listen, and pressed PLAY.

> He imagined that his memoirs might now sound like those of an admirable stranger, a person he did not know but whom he immediately recognized and loved dearly. Instead, the voice he

1. November 5, 1837.

heard sounded nasally and pinched and, worse, not very well educated, as if he were a bumpkin who had been called, perhaps even in mockery, to testify about holy things, as if not the testimony but the fumbling through it were the reason for his presence in front of some dire, heavenly senate. He listened to six seconds of the tape before he ejected it and threw it into the fire burning in the woodstove.[2]

There is an admirable stranger in my story: not me, but the God who almost never crossed my mind. I suspect—in fact, I am quite sure—that God doesn't wait for some kind of grownup decision or conscious choice to get involved with us; God doesn't stay offstage until we bow in prayer, learn Bible stories, endure boring worship services, or head off to a Christian retreat. God loves subtlety, dabbling behind the scenes—and God is pleased when we finally notice, when we remember, when we are struck from behind.

I certainly can't bear the thought of God as the orchestrator of events so the plot of my life would unfold according to some plan. I do not believe God has had some "plan" for my life—for to believe such is to stumble into the ugly notion that God inflicts harm or the shrinkage of soul, or makes family discord happen, that God breaks your heart to drive you toward God, and worst of all that God kills people you love and need quite desperately.

So where is God in my crowded little cottage of memory? If I can discern a gracious, unasked for goodness from God in my hazy recollection, am I merely projecting? Or in search of healing? Are the facts even straight? I suspect that while God is a stickler for truth, God doesn't mind if in my reminiscing I idealize or understandably falsify a little. Who can go back and check these things? If I unintentionally distort a fact or two, I still hope to remember God rightly.

St. Augustine, the pioneer in this endeavor to recall God through memories of times God was not noticed or invoked, spoke to his forgotten and then remembered Lord:

> Behold, how far within my memory have I traveled in search of you, Lord, and beyond it I have not found you! Nor have I found anything concerning you except what I have kept in memory since I first learned of you . . . But where within my memory do you abide, Lord, where do you abide? What kind of abode have you fashioned for yourself? What manner of sanctuary have

2. Paul Hardin, *Tinkers* (New York: Bellevue Literary Press, 2008), 22.

you built for yourself? So great an honor have you given to my memory as to abide within it. In what part of it you abide, this do I now consider.[3]

I have written this memoir largely for myself, to help me fill out my own story, to read between the lines and discover what I had missed. I also write for you, so as you look over my shoulder and overhear what I have begun to learn about God, you will remember God from your own life. I don't assume my life is all that interesting. But life is interesting, and God is downright fascinating.

Now that I've sat still long enough to remember things, I find my life to be a surprising treasure, heartbreaking, delightful, sad, funny, and above all worth having lived. As I have read what I have written, I can confess to you that I have cried more than I dreamed I would—reminding me of the day J. R. R. Tolkien wrote the climactic scene in his *Lord of the Rings*. His own tears spilled onto the paper as he wrote of the welcome of Frodo and Sam, the heroic hobbits, on the Field of Cormallen.

I hope you might let loose a few tears, and perhaps even more chuckles as you read. Instead of a long, year by year chronicle of happenings, I have organized these recollections topically. The first chapter, on my earliest childhood, was the hardest to tell, and not only because so many years have passed. Chapter 10 is about gifts I've received and given, involving a couple of pocket knives, a Lionel train set, and really the worst gift ever that turned out quite well.

Speaking of the best gifts, I will tell you about falling in love in chapter 4, from awkward romantic disasters to my lucky marriage, and then in chapter 5 about all the ways God has shown up to me in family fun, goofs and pain. Speaking of pain, chapter 6 focuses on what I've seen happen in hospitals, those numbing griefs and deaths that made standing erect difficult, and God's apparent absences; but then in chapter 7 I share the story of one miracle cure, and another astonishing miracle, even though it wasn't the cure we'd prayed for.

I devote two chapters (11 and 12) to travel, trying to explain my devotion to ruins, and also recounting the strangest and most compelling people I've met, from a gypsy to a Lithuanian banshee—and a nocturnal meeting with St. Francis in his hometown. My dad's hometown, Oakboro, was so resplendent in my memory that an entire chapter is devoted to my time with grandparents, idyllic yes, but no less real.

---

3. *The Confessions of St. Augustine*, translated by John K. Ryan (Garden City, NY: Image, 1960), 253 (*Confessions* X.24.35).

Introduction

There's a section on reading, and how books have blown uncountable hours and dollars while ushering God into my consciousness, and another on how I came to faith—the twin centerpieces of that chapter being the Baptists trying to kill me, and Jesus speaking to me in the night.

You can read in any order. The secret isn't the order, or the logic of the linear passing of time. Dates get jumbled; the name of the guy I spoke with three days ago, I can't recall, but then the immediacy of sitting at a table with friends thirty five years ago is palpable. Jesus did teach us to remember him at a meal that happened some time ago, and in the commonality of the everyday, eating bread, drinking wine. "Do this in remembrance of me." I like to think he might also have meant "Remember your life in remembrance of God."

Chapter 1

Little Brother
Slides & Fractures

STANDING IN THE STREET called Cofield Drive, where my parents built their "dream house," the dream shattered by endless arguments and eventual divorce, I realized a woman on the inside was eyeing me through the window. Lest she phone the police, I walked up and rang the bell. She peered through the cracked open door and heard me say "I'm sorry to bother you. My name is James Howell, and I lived here when I was growing up."

"Howell? Oh, yes, we bought this house from your parents in 1974. Would you like to come in?" Well, of course I wanted to come in. We stood a little bit awkwardly in the kitchen, and then the den. Her husband didn't rise from the couch; she told me he was suffering congestive heart failure.

"Which room was yours?" I pointed down the hall: "The one on the left." "Why don't you go to your room?" My parents had made this same suggestion many times, but with an entirely different intonation. I walked into a place that, as I should have suspected, was surprisingly small. Then, rather wonderfully, she asked, "Could I bring you some milk and cookies?" Had God devised this whimsical blessing for me when this couple saw a house back in 1974 and wanted to buy it?

Why had I driven to this street in the first place, parked the car, gotten out and stared long enough to look conspicuous? What was I hoping to find, or remember—or realize? I wish I had thought to pray, or even think about God, but I confess I did not—just as I had not when I'd lived there. Perhaps my search in some subterranean realm was a seeking after God, or at least what God promises people like me.

Struck from Behind

After my sister and I were grown, and my parents divorced, I happened to become the possessor of the cardboard box of slides, and also the old projector, the kind you manually operated, ka-chinking the Kodachrome diapositives into the hot casing where a bright bulb cast images onto a bare wall, the box advancing gradually. Since the projector didn't function any longer, and you couldn't buy bulbs or parts any more, I would retrieve one slide and then another, holding each up to the light, squinting to see what moments they had captured: those visits to grandparents or the beach, the vacations to Charleston and Marineland, the inevitable, embarrassing bathtub shots, birthday cakes and Christmas trees.

Eventually I paid a professional to transform them into digital images. Now they reside in my computer, where occasionally I rifle through a few when I'm by myself. Why would anybody else be interested? I do recall little family gatherings: we would turn out the lights and look at—well, at ourselves, our journeys, our high moments.

Somehow the slides are happier than my memory, the generalized mood I feel when I think back to being four or eleven. The camera demands "cheese," and of course we would never point a camera at unhappiness, or quarrels. We had too much of both. And yet my childhood somehow manages to persist for me as what Rilke called "that precious, kingly possession, that treasure-house of memories."[1]

Fractured Skull

One of the slides shows my sister, known back then as Janet, posing next to a fairly hokey, life-size wax figure of Babe Ruth—entirely fitting, since she

---

1. Rainer-Maria Rilke, *Letters to a Young Poet*, trans. M. D. Herter Norton (New York: Norton, 1934), 20.

was a slugger. So I drift back in my mind to the afternoon when my sister the slugger fractured my skull.

I'd been warned: Don't get too close. But what four- year-old has any restraint? And how could I comprehend how much peril there could be, right in my own backyard, and at the hands of my big sister? My only sibling's prowess with a baseball bat was legendary in our neighborhood. As an eight-year-old, she—yes, *she*, back in the 1950s when girls were supposed to be prissy—could hit the ball a mile. I kept edging too near home plate, a makeshift piece of cardboard in the dirt.

Everyone saw it coming—everyone except me, that is. The pitch, the swing—and thus the bat caught me in the forehead, and I was instantly plunged into total darkness. More than five decades later, scans still reveal a crack, the aftermath of Janet's Ruthian swing.

The curious, sad, but hopeful oddity is that this moment stands out as one of my fondest memories. How could a skull fracture count as one of the happiest days? My surprise, when I recall that lazy and then panicked afternoon decades ago, is that I *mattered*: I was hauled with an urgent fury by my dad to a hospital, while my sister was being chewed out (or worse). The story of a childhood should not unfold in this way: oh, on *that* afternoon, when that awful thing happened, *then* I mattered. Did I think they would just leave me sprawled behind home plate? Or scold me harshly for getting too close? Maybe?

You see, if I was a precious, kingly, treasured child, I was not aware of it—or was terribly unsure. I was very, very small. Physically, I was always frail, sickly, shorter and skinnier than everybody else. More importantly, there were a thicket of emotional forces which made me feel even smaller. Neither my mother nor my father would surrender in their long, dispiriting war with one another, or rise up out of their own inner quandaries—which I think left me with a kind of brokenness in the head. I can understand, and even sympathize in a way with my parents, whose passions were consumed in their own marital battles. But understanding isn't a cure, and sympathy most decidedly is not a rewind button so you can redo a different childhood.

At times I felt barely visible, sometimes wishing I could become invisible—and yet feared I might just shrink and disappear, and no one would notice. I've always thought that one day I'd shed this sense of smallness. But through my working and married life, the rattling around of belittling messages in my head has plagued me, and simultaneously driven me (unhealthily, I presume).

3

Struck from Behind

Because of this, I am someone with a native understanding of my need for that cluster of unearned wonders we luck into now and then: friendship, or love, or the fellowship that is the church and the hope it preaches, or the grace of God—the best definition of which may be, quite simply, *You matter*. And I find a tenacious fondness in me for the miraculous wonder that God became small for us, and that right after birth, Jesus found himself in some peril. He made it, and I made it—maybe like Cain in the Bible, who had an awful tussle with a sibling, and spent the rest of his days with an indelible imprint of God's reprieve on his head. I like it when my forehead gets marked on Ash Wednesday. The fracture: a curious sign of grace.

Big Sister

Back to my only sibling, the one who nearly killed me. Jann—well, she was born as Janet, went by Jan, then added an *n* in adulthood, I think trying to grow beyond the swirl of a traumatic life as either Janet or Jan. Life really was harder for her. The oldest shoulders the heavy loads first. And I recall quite clearly the message that it was a boy my parents had really wanted. I was that boy, so I enjoyed some sunshine and Jann was left in the dark. Jann is the epitome of what we often discover: those who have been wounded are the ones who know how to love, to include others who are hurting.

To Jann, there has never been such a thing as a "stray," for stray dogs and people are welcome in her home, always. She has become something of an animal whisperer, a Dr. Doolittle who can talk to the animals (whether they are among the quick or the dead!). Next to her I feel like a chicken. I'm not sure I am a timid, fearful person, but I was paralyzed by sheer terror one night when my parents' arguing spun out of control. My bedroom door was ajar. I heard shouting—and out of her room sprinted my sister, leaping into the fray to break it up. I never budged, too scared, too little, too uncertain about what I should even to try to do.

Jann's most unfortunate number might have been 1952—the year of her birth. Had she been born in, let's say 1987, like my first daughter, much about her being in the world would have been happier, and more admired. Jann was, beyond question, the best athlete, not just in our house, but on the whole block, in the entire neighborhood, probably in the whole school system. She could hit a ball harder and farther than anybody; she had a strong arm, great instincts, a nose for the ball—but she was this terrific athlete in an era that giggled over the notion of girls playing a sport, and looked askance at a girl who happened to be, and dared to be . . . good.

At first guys weren't sure whether to say her name when choosing sides for softball or football. But after getting trounced a few times, they figured things out, and she was always the first chosen. I was in the stands when our school had its annual, absurdly silly "powder puff" football game, when cute girls squealed, ran about like sissies, primped their sprayed hair, attempted awkward passes that sailed three yards—you get the picture. Jann ran the opening kickoff back for a touchdown, then picked off an errant pass and ran it into the end zone, then ran for another score: three touches, three touchdowns. A solemn Mrs. Prissy-something-or-another sternly walked onto the field and told Jann she couldn't play any longer.

Knowing her athletic prowess, and that my parents (like all the mothers and fathers in the Bible!) wanted a boy, a friend of mine once suggested she became that boy. But that is precisely the injustice writ large in our psyches! God made her strong, agile, with extraordinary hand-eye coordination—and it wasn't the first or last time God did something lovely and nobody quite understood.

It occurs to me that, because of my life with my sister, I woke up to the social justice dimensions of the life of faith before any apprehension of God proper dawned on me. In college, I would be transfixed by C. S. Lewis's *Mere Christianity*, where his logical case for the faith begins with "right and wrong as a clue to the meaning of the universe." I am not disappointed in retrospect that I discerned strong feelings about what was just and unjust first—and only later came to know the God who authored the right and wrong, and fashioned us in God's "image," which must be the fire in us that cares, gets riled up, and fights back.

Subverting Stereotypes

Jann clashed with authority the way most people stand and smile glibly at a party. We sometimes attended a Southern Baptist church in our neighborhood, and Jann offered to provide music for a Sunday night service. But when she showed up with her friend, Cynthia, she was told by an usher that they couldn't come in because Cynthia was black—a "negro" in those days, although the usher may have used that cruder, meaner spelling we heard too often from pious but mean people our parents' age.

Psychologists have processed a lot of data about birth order and sibling rivalry. I wonder what role older siblings play in social and moral awakenings? The older sibling gets there first. The younger one looks up, watches, and wonders. I'm cheering like crazy for my sister—and she's ejected for scoring touchdowns? I'm eager to hear my sister and her friend sing some religious song about the Jesus who embraced nobodies, shattered barriers, and even (as I was beginning to believe) cared something about me; but then Cynthia, whose skin color I now understand was probably closer to Jesus's than my sister's, can't get in the door? You've never had to convince me to be a rabble-rouser, a demonstrator, to stand up for what's good and right, because early on I couldn't help but notice the blatant absurdity of gender backwardness and racial bigotry.

I endured a bit of such nonsense myself. In ninth grade, my mother forced me, against my will, to take typing, which in those days was housed in that antiquated, feminine wing of the building, the Home-Ec department. A roomful of old manual peck peck, ka-ching return Royal typewriters, perched before a couple of dozen girls and . . . me. Disgraceful enough, but as it turned out I was good at typing, probably because I'd been forced also to take piano lessons; my digital dexterity gave me an edge on timed tests.

At the end of the school year, the student body was massed in the assembly hall for awards day. I was not really paying attention when I thought I heard my name through the loudspeaker system, "James Howell," followed by a chorus of snickering. I had won—what? The typing award? Not only boys but also girls found this to be quite amusing.

And then the chuckles erupted into convulsions when I was handed the award itself: a charm bracelet. Evidently the awards had been purchased years in advance, before the winners were named, and obviously before the securer could imagine that a boy might excel in typing. So there I stood, dishonored, utterly humiliated, the epitome of infamy. I wished some trap door on the stage had opened and I could have tumbled, unseen, all the way to China. Two or three years later, I would still pass bullies in the hallway who would mockingly inquire, "Hey James, wearing your charm bracelet today?"

I put up with additional jeering because kids also knew I played the piano, which in those days was still the domain of girls, a piece of their "finishing," I believe. I put up with the taunting—but now I know who got the last laugh. Sure, they snickered at me—but years later I had an enormous advantage when I courted young women who, as it turned out, couldn't play the piano but swooned over the fact that I could. God loves this sort of reversal of roles, and the way the ridiculous over time becomes truly lovely.

So you can certainly understand why I am puzzled and then get agitated when I hear who can do what and who can't because of gender—and especially in the church. I was supposed to play ball—but I could type? Jann could clobber a softball—but she couldn't be a pastor? Cynthia could sing like an angel—but she couldn't even sit in the back? I could play the piano—but could I preach? Yes, the Bible is God's word, and a flatfooted reading of it might suggest I should be an alpha male and Jann should be demure. But God's word was heard and then written down by people sharp and yet thoughtless, and surely as swept up in their own day's cultural *mores* as the usher, the woman presiding over powder puff, the typing teacher, and even me, my sister, and the rest of us.

When I was a Q

An athletic girl born in 1952 was trouble—inversely matched to the woefulness of my being an utterly unathletic boy born in 1955. October 22 of 1955, that is—an alarmingly late birthday, casting me forever as the smallest in my grade, and the last eventually to shave, or drive. I recall being thought of as smart. I didn't feel smart; it felt like a curse, one more reason to be shoved around by the bullies. Perhaps this brightness, which I wanted to hide or apologize for, was the hidden hope.

I did come to appreciate the cleverness that is the sophomoric side of intelligence. I skated through school with little effort, needing chicanery and some narrow escapes when a lack of discipline worked me into desperate corners. Most adults thought me a good, safe boy, although I've always been an under-the-radar rulebreaker. My dad was out of town on my fifteenth birthday, so I drove myself to the Highway Department, flunked the drivers' license test, and then drove myself back home. I like it that the Bible seems so fond of rogues like Jacob who don't take the sidewalk but cut across the grass despite the signs.

The rule I couldn't skirt was that short, skinny, clumsy boys were the unchosen when sides were picked for kickball. Trying but failing miserably to be inconspicuous (or, even more absurdly, daring to pretend to be a desirable team member), I would sit, hoping not to be the last name called, cringing as girls got picked ahead of me. As an adult, if I drive by a random school playground, I shudder a little, as the memory of a repeated scene from childhood is evoked: I walk up to a little band of kids, who would then flip out with hilarity, and hurl some insult my way—often using a word that I didn't even know the meaning of, further underlining my imbecility.

"Q!" That was the single letter a handful of boys kept shouting my way when I was in third grade. I had no clue what Q might signify, but I knew it was vicious. I wonder if young Jesus had such difficulties. One of those early gospels that didn't make it into the Bible, "The Infancy Gospel of Thomas," regales us with a far-fetched story: a playmate poked fun at Jesus one day. Wielding not playground kid power, but divine power, Jesus waved his finger and struck the boy dead. But he was God, so he had no choice but to be filled with remorse. So he deployed that same power that struck the boy dead to raise him back to the land of the living. I don't accept this fiction that Jesus struck vicious playmates down; but I do wonder if Jesus felt the kind of angst, awkwardness, or even shame I felt. If the adult Jesus battled rejection and suffered much, why do all the pastel, corny artist renderings of Jesus as a child portray him as cute and gleeful? What degrading names was Jesus called?

Had I been granted Bruce Almighty-like divine power, I would have struck a few kids down and left them for the vultures. On second thought, if I'd had divine power, I would have cast some spell and made them play with me and pick me first for kickball, and maybe love me—but what was Aladdin's lesson? Even a genie can't make somebody love you. God can't and won't force the love.

Having been dubbed (for no other reason than being short, or a lousy kickball player, or maybe for my hair being greasy) a Q, I came over the years to surmise Q must have devolved from the word "queer," which once upon a time meant, well *queer*, as in, *a bit strange*. But before my childhood was done, not only "queer" but also "gay" came to stand for sexual orientation. In my denomination, as in society at large, we've argued endlessly, with far more venom and emotional fervor than wisdom or receptiveness, about the theological meaning of homosexuality. I've never felt personally vexed that a guy might like a guy, or a woman a woman. The biblical and theological issues are vexing. For some time I harbored the fantasy that I would be the one to be a modern day William Wilberforce, to do for homosexuality what he did for slavery, that I would definitively resolve the theological argument. I've not gotten that done.

Having been snickered at so many times, I have tried to stand with those misunderstood and judged. As a boy, I wished I had been able to fight the boys who humiliated me; in adult life I have made it my purpose to fight for the cause of the dignity of the unwanted or shunned, although I fear my effectiveness has not risen far above my kickball abilities. I have found myself quite readily on the "side" of the gays and lesbians, although the very idea of "sides" is appalling.

I shall never forget the first time I ever heard of a Q spoken of affirmatively. At first I had advocated openness in the church for gays and lesbians. And I can admit to a touch of uneasiness when LG grew to LGBT. *Let the conservatives adjust to LG first! and then, maybe someday, they might warm to Bs and Ts,* or so I thought.

And then the day came someone told me a fifth letter had been added: LGBTQ! Q? I knew that one. I'd been a Q for a full decade of childhood. So yes, absolutely, I will stand with the Qs. It is not pleasing to God when anybody has to be endlessly defensive, and no matter how hard you try to prove yourself, you never quite arrive, and the self is crushed. As a southern boy I was supposed to be a strapping ballplayer, and a car mechanic to boot. But there I was, skinny, no agility, a piano player—pretty strange, "queer" being an accurate term after all.

Cures of Dysfunction

Having done time on the playground, and then also at home, I think I'm far more easily persuaded than others that I desperately need God. The Bible has come to be of immense comfort to me, because the families portrayed in its pages are every bit as messy and dysfunctional as that broken down foursome we Howells were. Cain was jealous of Abel and clobbered him. Jacob and Esau battled in the womb, and once out either enjoyed or were infuriated by the divided partialities of their parents. Jacob had his favorites, sparking a civil war among his sons. David couldn't get marriage right, and his sons fought not only with each other but with David himself. How good of God to give us such scriptures! What if all the Bible families were Ozzie and Harriet happy, peaceful, grinning, pious, and sugary sweet to one another? God had to know that such a bland, hokey Bible with such glib images would ostracize the rest of us, and tempt the happy families toward self-righteousness.

It is hard to think of a mere book, much less a virtual fossil of a book like the Bible, being a great solace—and if all we had was a book, we would never believe in God. There were other signs of great grace besides the Bible before I even knew how to read the thing. There was an older couple, George and Ann Mauney, who were neighbors in Savannah. For reasons even my parents haven't been able to explain to me, Jann and I wound up spending many nights in their home. Ann was large of spirit and jolly in temperament, George crustier but great fun. He nicknamed me "Pistol," although I do not know why—and a certain unmentionable body part was referred to as "Trigger." I loved that.

I do not know what happened to them, but when I was three, and six, they provided a warm womb of respite from our colder, more dispiriting residence. Theirs was much affection and laughter, and Jann and I were loved by them because . . . well, I don't think there is any *because*, or if there were a because (maybe they were lonely, or owed my dad some money; something nefarious would be titillating now, wouldn't it?) I think I prefer not to know. Two grown people who had no obligation to love us loved us. Isn't that the grace of God in bodily form?

If you ask me about tangible grace, and how I can conceive of God as Father (or as Jesus once invited us to imagine things, God as the Mother gathering her brood), and of church as a tender family, I skip a generation beyond my immediate family and reminisce, with pleasure and gratitude, about my grandparents.

Chapter 2

Oakboro
Mama & Papa Howell

IF MY PARENTS HAD written memoirs, or even if they had reminisced more, revealing sorrowful or joyful stories from their own childhoods, I might have understood them better. Perhaps they could have understood themselves better, and maybe even enjoyed more seasons of happiness, and that their world, and thus my world, would have been sunnier, or healthier. But who can know?

I wonder if their view of their parents matches my view of their parents, my grandparents, who have provided prodigious blessing, and a twist of weirdness. The latter would come from my maternal grandparents. My mother's mother was only a black and white photo to me. Cancer had felled her before I was born. I know my mother had an unalloyed devotion to her mother, whom she tenderly called "Mama," full of gratitude and yet regret she left her far too soon. My mother's father I tried to love, but could not connect. He played a wiry, out of tune guitar, and dipped snuff. He had never installed a bathroom in his tiny un-airconditioned house. When we visited and needed to "go," we had to tiptoe back to an outhouse, with stench, flies, and bees.

My grandfather would put me in his old truck, and then amble up a bumpy dirt road punctuated by potholes to a little white clapboard country store. He would emerge with a brown paper bag, from which he would drink, not bringing me anything, not offering the bag or its mystical contents either. Who knows what his history might have been, or his with my mother. I know I was never sorry when trips to his shack ended, and his funeral was a numb sort of relief, I'm sorry to admit.

Struck from Behind

At Home in Oakboro

But if you ask me to rank my fondest childhood memories, and if you ask me how God was there, I zoom immediately in to my *other* grandparents: my father's parents, Nezzie and Artus Howell—whom we affectionately called Mama and Papa Howell. "Affectionately" would be an understatement. I can declare with total objectivity that they were the finest, most loving and wonderful grandparents any child has ever had. Argue with me on behalf of your own if you wish, but I will never concede—and simultaneously suggest that instead of arguing with me you should simply fall on your knees and give thanks to God.

There is a profound theological meaning in people like grandparents or your parent's home town, if you are blessed to know such loveliness. I spent most of my childhood summers in Oakboro—all summer long! What could they have been thinking when they took me and my sister in for so long? Oakboro, a little town with one traffic light (with the colors upside down): to get there, drive through Locust, hang a right at Frog Pond, bear left at Big Lick, and there it is, the sloping cemetery on the right, then the skating rink, the old school on the left, the filling station, a few small stores, then houses where various Howell kin have lived. My temporary, periodic home there was more home than my other home.

My grandparents were poor, uneducated people, yet dignified, devout in the best possible way, solid, admired citizens—but none of that really matters. They loved me; I mattered to them. When I would be deposited on their step, they would rejoice, and sweep me up in loving arms. When I would leave, they appeared to be sad. Papa Howell had this little liturgy of departure: we would be stashed in the car, my dad would back out of the driveway, and begin to accelerate toward that lone traffic light down the road. As if suddenly remembering what he'd forgotten, Papa Howell would hurry toward the car, imploring us to stop. I would roll down the window, he would reach in his pocket, and press into my palm a fifty-cent piece. In those days, my monthly allowance was fifty cents, so I needed this kind of money—but I never ever spent a single one of those precious gems. To this day, when I stand in a line and a priest presses a piece of bread into my hand, I recall the little gifts of Papa Howell. He was giving me money, in a way—but really he was giving himself; he wanted me to be able to clutch a piece of him with me when I was far from him. Maybe in the same way, Jesus knew little pieces of bread could bear the fullness of his entire being and guarantee we'd remember him after he was gone.

I didn't know it at the time, but I learned the meaning of theological vocation from Papa Howell (although nobody in Oakboro used hifalutin terms like "theological" or "vocation"). He was a rural mail carrier. I think he sensed that this was what God placed him on earth to do, and he worked at it as if on a mission from God, dispensing kindness with the mail, delivering medicine and groceries along with postal packages, stopping at times to pray with persons along the way. I know; he took me with him many times. He could have landed a better job somewhere else. But he had a keen sense of his crucial place in the functioning of the small town of Oakboro, North Carolina.

The Beauty of Loss

Now I have his desk, his mail pouch, and his Bible—just things, but they convey his presence decades after his passing. How did he pass, you ask? The night is still clear in my mind. The telephone rang—one of those "burglar alarms of the heart," as John Irving aptly described such calls. My dad, or perhaps my mother, shook us out of bed. *Hurry! Now!—he's very ill.* Papa Howell, the epitome of whatever delight and goodness filled my childhood, my hero and best friend, so ill that my aunt phoned at such an hour: we piled into the car and drove hard for hours, silently, along the road we had traversed so many times filled with playful anticipation.

Not long after dawn, we finally pulled up in front of the house. My sister and I didn't move; the word "petrified" seems about right. My father turned off the car, opened the door, and walked up to his brothers, who were standing under the giant oak tree where we had all played and churned ice cream a hundred times. My sister and I could not hear what was said, but we saw my dad and his brothers fall on each other's shoulders, and they cried out loud. This was in the mid-sixties, and my dad and uncles were all strong, military men not easily moved to tears.

My saddest, but perhaps my most beautiful moment: the death of my beloved Papa Howell, knee-buckling, yet beautiful. For in that moment we children learned that life is precious, that love is intense, that a life could matter so much. There is a beauty hidden in grief. Love unfailingly plunges you into excruciating agony. But we would not think for a moment of loving any less.

We could say "God's love is like that," and so it is. God's love costs God and costs us everything, and tears are shed. But the gospel is not merely illustrated by this moment of my grandfather's death. God was under those trees and in my gut, as God is always palpable when God's children suffer but manage to stand and take another breath. In grown men's sobbing we overhear God's own lament. In a child's stricken agony we are enveloped by the heart of God.

Mama Howell lived a few sad years past his death, through days of illness, pain, and I think much loneliness, despite the tender care of family. Papa and Mama Howell live in me; they are the grace of God rippling through my vascular system, populating my head with happy thoughts, girding me to believe in myself.

Faith Healer

Recollection of grace can do that to you. Under that same old oak tree where my father and his brothers wept, we used to churn ice cream in the lengthening afternoon shade. Mama Howell would prepare her milk, peach, chocolate, and sugar concoction. My sister would shimmy chunks of ice down into the perimeter of the churn, lacing the ice with salt. Papa Howell would sit on a little wooden chair and turn the crank.

One evening, I was surprised, eager, and a little hesitant when Papa Howell summoned me to the task: "Whew, I'm gettin' a little tired . . . James, come over here and help me." He hoisted me over his knee and onto his lap. I cockily grasped the handle, and pushed with all my might. His hand rested on mine, strongly, helping in that gentle way that you don't notice until you're grown, turning, turning, turning again, the voice of praise right in my ear, "Good job, good job." Grace and truth, and from behind.

Seminary taught me formal prayers to unfurl in a hospital room, but my grandfather taught me how to be a faith healer. When I would get the hiccups, my aunts, uncles, and cousins would ply me with foolish remedies until he arrived home. "Hiccups? I know just the thing." He would lift me up, and situate me on his lap, facing forward, straddling his legs—and then (behind me again) he commenced with a voodoo series of taps and bumps from his fingers and fists up and down my back, a pattern of here, there, harder, softer . . . and the hiccups vanished every time. His cure worked, I know now, because I had faith in the healer.

Somewhat hilariously, I found myself years later, knowing precisely what to do when my own children complained of their inevitable hiccups. A spoonful of sugar? Holding your breath? Sipping water upside down from a glass? I waved off such ineffectual antidotes, and confidently placed Sarah or Grace or Noah on my lap, back toward me, and began the patterned thumps. Hiccups cured!—and I revealed to them I learned this medicine from Papa Howell. If my children have their own children one day, I trust they will know what to do.

Mama Howell was holy in a different way. Although they were poor, she dressed every day, and took great pride in her jewelry, hats, and shoes. And yet when my sister and I would get into her closet and dress up, she never seemed to mind. Her room was adorned with paintings that mimicked Degas: those pretty, elegant ballet dancers. She knew and appreciated beauty, although she could not afford many beautiful things. Her real treasures, we at least believed, were her grandchildren.

Struck from Behind

One day my sister and I had a little contest in that room with the Degas prints. We climbed onto her old sewing machine, the kind with a flat pedal that operated the needle, to see who could make it go up and down the fastest. Jann went first, and pedaled rapidly, the needle whirring away. My turn came, and I pressed even harder, the needle a mere blur. Not to be outdone, she shoved me off the bench and began bicycling the thing herself even more recklessly—and then an unanticipated voice interrupted our lunacy: "Children?" We turned, mortified. If your parents catch you doing such things, you are scolded and punished. But it was Mama Howell, and she knew how to handle such hoodlums: "Children? I just pulled some peach cobbler out of the oven; don't you want to come get some?" Isn't God's grace, not scolding or correcting, but luring us toward something more wonderful than whatever it is God calls us away from?

She hummed and occasionally whistled old hymns as she cooked, swept, knitted, or rocked. And there was always room at her small table for one more—a passerby who happened to be in the yard around mealtime, a cousin at loose ends, a laborer with time on his hands. Years later I envisioned Mama Howell when I read Dorothy Day's recollection and counsel: "Let's all try to be poorer. My mother used to say, 'Everyone take less, and there will be room for one more.' There was always room for one more at our table."[1]

The Hands of Christ

And there were others in Oakboro: my great grandmother who was spry and funny into her late nineties, my Down syndrome cousin Sharon who was always the happiest of us all, able to be content with a few shiny coins in a cheap purse, my Uncle Famon who raised cows, pigs and chickens, and of course my Aunt Zonia. I suppose my grandparents wearied of me at times, so I would get farmed out to others in town—and I loved staying with my great Aunt Zonia.

I'm unsure how an orthopedist would diagnose my aunt, but her hands were gnarled, underdeveloped somehow, fairly useless, awkward. You would think, "Oh, those are not good hands, they must be a problem." One night, a stiff fever and awful nausea laid me low. In my misery, Aunt Zonia stayed with me all night long, and with her twisted fingers she took a cold cloth and wiped my brow. She could have held back, thinking "Oh,

1. Jim Forest, *Love is the Measure: A Biography of Dorothy Day*, rev. ed. (Maryknoll, NY: Orbis, 1994), 135.

my hands are bad hands, I wish I had soft, supple fingers instead of these cramped digits." But she took my small hands in her hands as best she could, and she didn't let go.

As a little boy, I discovered another hidden beauty in her hands. Returning home from the grocery store, she couldn't carry the bags into the house. She really needed me. No pretending: I was important at Aunt Zonia's house. I had a skill that made a difference. An odd quartet of hands the two of us shared: I could serve this woman who had served me.

Years passed, and she phoned me from the hospital. I found her in intensive care, where she lay with a brain tumor, not expected to live long at all. Proud that I had grown up to be a man of the cloth, she asked "Will you preach my funeral? And will you pray for me?" I took her hands, or perhaps it was she who took mine, and we prayed. We offered her up to God.

I've always been fond of the notion that we are the hands of Christ. The most remarkable hands I've ever been involved with, and therefore the hands that must be most like Christ's hands, were Aunt Zonia's. To be Christ's hands isn't about being pretty, or strong, or dexterous. Christ's hands touch as best they can, a little awkwardly but no less lovingly because of it. And Christ's hands don't do all the heavy lifting, but trust other hands to do some picking up and carrying themselves.

A Better Place

When I think back on the meaning of my life with my grandparents in that modest yet glorious town of Oakboro, I think of something Allan Bloom wrote about real learning, and also something Marilynne Robinson wrote about this world and the world to come. First, Bloom's words on his grandparents (and more fittingly, my own):

> My grandparents were ignorant people by our standards, and my grandfather held only lowly jobs. But their home was spiritually rich because all the things done in it . . . found their origin in the Bible's commandments, and their explanations in the Bible's stories. I do not believe that my generation, my cousins who have been educated in the American way, all of whom are M.D.s or Ph.D.s, have any comparable learning. When they talk about heaven and earth, the relations between men and women,

> parents and children, the human condition, I hear nothing but
> clichés, superficialities, the material of satire.[2]

There is a touch of cynical nostalgia in Bloom's assessment. But my grand-parents most certainly knew how to talk about heaven, children, and things that mattered. They were truly wealthy. Because of them, I enjoyed a spiritually rich home away from home.

Even more hopefully, Robinson thought of the way we say someone who has died has "gone to a better place." She knows, as we do, that a grander locale waits for us—and yet . . .

> I can't believe that, when we have all been changed and put on incorruptibility, we will forget our fantastic condition of mortal-ity and impermanence, the great bright dream of procreating and perishing that mean the whole world to us. In eternity this world will be Troy, I believe, and all that has passed here will be the epic of the universe, the ballad they sing in the streets. Because I don't imagine any reality putting this one in the shade entirely, and I think piety forbids me to try.[3]

Could it be that the function of a place away from home, a second home, with beloved grandparents, infusing so much grace and shimmering with love and belonging, might be to help us know how to think about a longed-for home, "not made with hands, but eternal in the heavens," so we might believe, and yearn, and even be patient in the waiting? Do we believe in a better place because we've spent time in . . . a better place?

The Howell Family Game

And how do we live in the meantime, while we are in this waiting mode? When we would have our family reunions, usually as close to Christmas as possible, we would crowd into Aunt Wadene's basement and play a game. I thought it was uniquely "the Howell game," although years later I learned it was a quite common gift exchange game, where you draw numbers: #1 selects a gift, and then subsequent number drawers can "steal" the gifts of others. None of the gifts were anything great, like a car or a stereo or a mink coat, but just ridiculous trinkets, the more ridiculous the better, the funnier. You learned the rules, you played patiently and with many smiles, and whatever you went home with was simply what you got, the benefit

2. Allan Bloom, *The Closing of the American Mind* (New York: Simon & Schuster, 1987), 60.

3. Marilynne Robinson, *Gilead* (New York: Farrar Straus and Giroux, 2004), 57.

of the game being in the love, the laughter, the joy of belonging in such a wonderful, cozy place as Wadene's basement, and the womb of this family. The following year we would do it again.

I cannot think of a more profound image of the life of the Body of Christ than this game. We Christians gather in a place, its modesty or grandeur being incidental to the joy of the event. We have some habits, some gestures we've learned over time. You get up out of your seat and are handed a gift—a ridiculously small trinket, a piece of bread. We speak words, openly admitting to our crimes—a confession to God of wayward-ness, yet one that never ever gets you ostracized from the family.

And it is all the same, year after year. Every year Christians, not get-ting bored but rather invigorated by the routine, redo their march from Advent through Epiphany, then Lent and Easter, Pentecost to Christ the King, and then we do it all over again, and again. Every week, we come into the sanctuary and do the same stuff we did just one week prior. An-nie Dillard tells about worshipping at a little church on Puget Sound; one week the minister, kneeling and leading the congregation in petitions from the *Book of Common Prayer*, suddenly stopped, looked up to the ceiling, and exclaimed, "Lord, we say these same prayers every week!" Dil-lard's impressions? "Because of this, I like him very much."[4] God hears us saying the same prayers every week, singing the same songs, hearing sermons that aren't so fresh or creative, muttering creeds and the Lord's Prayer—and God likes us very much because of this.

Sad thing about that Howell game: sometimes there would be one or two (often a new spouse or somebody who hadn't shown up for a long time) who refused to play. Their loss! and yet they were never given a thrashing, or humiliated, or forced to exit the basement. They still got des-sert, and couldn't go home without being hugged and told they were loved. The church always has those who won't play, or can't play. But we love, we hope they will join in one day.

Not to make too much of a silly game, but there are even more ways this game illustrates the life of the Body. I felt so special that we had our special game; but as it turns out, lots of families play, and in my working life my staffs have played, as have other staffs. The game isn't less special because somebody else plays! The joy widens, and each new playing re-kindles the memory of playing somewhere else, in some earlier decade.

When others play, there are slight aberrations in the rules. You can only steal a gift twice? What? Some churches just do things differently; their precise implementation of the gestures, the prayers and movements

4. Annie Dillard, *Holy the Firm* (New York: Harper & Row, 1977), 58.

differ a little. We can focus on the differences and get mad with one another, or we can relish the delight that at the end of the day we are all playing the same game.

And there's this: when you play the Howell game (or your office game if you'd prefer to think of it that way), you walk out with a gift, and the next person out the door has a very different gift. So it is with the Body of Christ. You got a knack for numbers and budgets? Cool! I can crochet prayer shawls. That guy over there is a great Bible teacher. But see her, behind him? She humbly labors behind the scenes and is happier there. Her mother is shut in and near death, but she prays for all of us.

Funny thing about the game: there is a humble courtesy that is the inviolable rule. If it was Uncle Leonard who got the prize plastic gizmo, nobody pouted or begrudged him the prize plastic gizmo. And if Aunt Croppsie was too frail to rise from her recliner, someone would bring her whatever she stole, and we all were especially tickled if the young cousin who'd had an awful year wound up with the much-desired fuzzy kangaroo. Don't we in the church rejoice with those who rejoice? And measure the quality of our life by how we care for those who are struggling?

Did the apostle Paul's family play this game? "There are varieties of gifts, but the same Spirit . . . The body does not consist of one member but of many . . . The eye cannot say to the hand, 'I have no need of you'. . . The parts of the body which seem to be weaker are indispensable . . . If one member is honored, all rejoice together" (1 Cor 12).

Had my dad actually grown up in this place, and among these people? My aunts assured me they remembered him as a very loving, tender, affectionate child, and I believe them. He was notorious for holding his breath until he passed out—maddeningly so in the eyes of his younger sisters and cousins. I am glad he was loving, and I take some hope from this shred of memory, and find myself hoping that some genetic passing down will materialize in me.

After all, I loved and love my father. There has been a distance we could never resolve. I'm not sure he could ever figure out who I was on the inside—and I effectively returned that favor. And yet it was his parents, and his home in Oakboro, which proved to be a safe, nurturing womb for me. He churned ice cream too, cried and laughed under the tree, there in Troy, a better place probably for him as for me. And although he was never much of a churchgoer, he had to have had glimpses of his own relationship with the same God who'd blessed me in that place, God *incognito* but no less vivid.

Chapter 3

Childhood Play
The Gift of Friendship

So in the slides and in the splotches of moments here and there that stick in my mind, I can discern faint traces of God lurking around, loving me, even luring me, patiently, perhaps speaking toward my deafness, whispering encouragement when I wasn't getting any from anybody else, certainly laughing God's own head off or moaning or most definitely shedding quite a few tears. For me, God isn't just a faint memory, but is the healing of memory, and the dream that surprising goods can emerge from awkwardness and sorrow. Playing with friends, falling in love, being confused, kicking a ball, getting a harsh whipping, and doing homework are all moments when the hidden God was there, even though the cast of characters would, back then, unanimously agree that God had not shown up or was not thought about. Prayers were not offered; God was not spoken of.

Beyond sorting things out, I like to dwell on childhood for theological reasons. My recollection of being very small gets me close to Jesus. Mary, Joseph, the shepherds, and the magi met Jesus when he was as little and vulnerable as I am in those old slides. If Jesus lived to be roughly thirty, then he spent half his life looking up—not to God so much as to people. He had to be fed, he was a dependent, he did what his mother told him to do; he was small, submissive. We need not romanticize childhood to realize that, when we rustle through the pages of the memories of our own early years, we are as close as we might get to feeling in some slight way what it might have been like for the Word to become flesh and dwell among us (John 1:14). What was that like for God? Jesus, once grown, called us "friends" (John 15:15); did he have friends when he was small?

The Gift of Friendship

What more lovely gift could any child have during the lazy, fleeting years of childhood than a playmate? I was lucky to have a few of them, and am grateful now to God for it. Only in seminary would I learn that Aristotle portrayed friendship as a school of virtue, and St. Augustine conceived of friendship as a way we might come to know God. We little boys did help each other to become good, to develop virtue, and even to grow toward God. Children who play learn to negotiate difficulties, and having fun is probably underrated in the kingdom's dull manifestation on earth, the church. Somebody cared enough to want me to spend the night at his house or to play stickball—so I began to believe I was a person of worth, who might one day realize God's eagerness to be with me.

How did I come to have the friends I had? A boy named David lived on the same block when I was in third grade, so that was easy. We moved during fourth grade, and somehow I stumbled upon a kid named Nick, who maybe was a neighbor, maybe just sat near me in school, or maybe he didn't really know anybody either.

But clearly my best, dearest, and intrinsically fun and wonderful childhood friend was Carl. We were in class together, but the attraction must have been that neither of us had athletic potential, neither of us was cool or popular, and both of us were viewed by our teachers as "smart," whatever that might have meant.

Although I have to give Carl 78 percent of the credit for the tomfoolery we got into, as he was more creative, or more confident, we did become quite the pair creating havoc for teachers. Simple spitballs were not sufficiently stimulating intellectually, so we fashioned various sizes and shapes, with coloration as best we could, and flung our drippy wet projectiles toward the ceiling, with startling success in our stated objective: to get them to stick and form a solar system above our heads. We tortured a poor Miz Stone (nobody used Ms. back then, but we pronounced every teacher's name as *Miz*, not knowing or caring if she were Miss or Mrs.), who in her fury determined we were to be paddled. She led us into the hallway, shut the door, but for unknown reasons laid her wooden paddle on a stool and stomped off (probably to the principal's office to let off steam). Eyeing our opportunity, we took turns with the paddle, whamming it into an old coat on the floor, after each whack emitting a loud yelp of pretended pain; then whamming it again into the stool or a locker or whatever was at hand, more screams flying. Miz Stone returned, relented, and led us back into the room, where our fellow students sat in petrified terror for the balance of the day.

Chemistry is a subject that must have been created for hooligans. We mixed this and that, making beakers smoke or turn odd shades of purple. We sprayed water from the sinks at one another. One day we followed a recipe and concocted some invisible gas that we took into the hallway and poured (the book assured us the gas was heavy and could in fact be "poured") a couple of gallons of the brew into a neighboring classroom through the dormer window. After a minute or two, kids were tumbling out of the room, sprinting to the bathroom, or simply surrendering to their coughing and nausea. Great fun. I like to think of God the creator as a kid in a chemistry lab who will stop at nothing, trying new combinations, mixing up batches of this and that to devise an endless array of wonders: a hermit crab and a crab nebula, a whippoorwill and a pterodactyl, volcanic lava and maple sap, and even me.

We hung out a lot, primarily at Carl's house, since my house was not a peaceful, welcoming place. I was grateful to be there, actually to be anywhere—but Carl's house was a wonder. The first time my dad took me there, he grew suspicious when we turned onto a road literally in the middle of nowhere. The prospects were not good as we drove a winding road through the woods—woods we could not have imagined that Carl's family owned. At the end was a large clearing, and then a Tara-style, picture-book home overlooking the Saluda River and downtown Columbia. Carl's family had hired help, a kindly woman who'd cook up some lunch at our request, and a gardener named Joseph who didn't believe astronauts really went to the moon: "They shot that in a TV studio, you know; it's impossible to go to the moon." But the Robertses did not behave like wealthy people. They were old money, humble people, and they treated me like a son and a brother.

When Carl and I would get in trouble, in fact, I was dumbfounded by his mother's response. My parents would have sided with any idiot teacher and blamed me every time. But Mrs. Roberts would assess things, talk to us about mistakes we may have made, and yet she was swift on a couple of occasions to stand and fight for us, to be an advocate for us against a petty-minded principal or teacher. We got suspended for our hair being too long—but Mrs. Roberts dragged us back to school, and fumed at the principal, clarifying that our hair was clean, and his rule was neither real nor rational. I'd never had anybody wield their power on my behalf before, and I liked it—and it's not hard to envision her by my side when I think about the Bible's insistence that "we have an Advocate in heaven" (1 John 2:1), that "if God is for us, who can be against us?" (Romans 8:31). And when I screw up my courage and take up someone's cause, it may be because I was a witness to, and a beneficiary of a childhood friend's mother.

The Beatles

The dominant images I have when I think of Carl and my childhood days are of the covers of the Beatles' albums which were by far my most treasured possessions. The Beatles became friends for life when I was still learning to have friends, and when they broke up I cried for days. I wish my brain had one of those computerized counters that could say "You have listened to *Let It Be* 2,937 times"—although the number I just made up might just be a bit low. Over and over, first with a transistor radio clutched near my ear, then sitting by my family's old turntable, later with 8 track tapes and then CDs, iPods and other gadgets, I have relistened to every song, I know every lyric by heart, have explored the divergent versions that came available years later—and have sung (in the car, shower, dorm room, and office) every song out loud, and played most on the piano.

Carl and I spent hours practicing the Beatles, he on the guitar, I on piano, finding harmonies we might sing. We entered a talent show in the ninth grade, sang "And I Love Her," and won $5, which Carl rather cleverly tore in half, kept his $2.50 worth and gave me the other. Tragically I have lost mine, but he still has his portion of the evidence of the true meaning of money. When I was in my fifties, I plunked down an unreasonable amount of cash for row 4 tickets to see Paul McCartney, and couldn't tell if I was laughing or crying when he came out on stage. I know I was crying the day John Lennon was shot outside the Dakota on the edge of Central Park, and George's death after his lingering cancer felt like the loss of a brother or close cousin.

Of course I've had other cultural attachments, never having been impressed by that insecure sort of Christian piety that trembles in fear or smugly passes judgment on all manifestations of culture that are not strictly pious (or even verge on impiety). I find I just like the Beatles, and even a lot of things that seem raunchy: the crass *Family Guy* cartoons I've even watched with my son, James Bond flicks, the zombies in *Walking*

Dead or Jack Bauer manhandling terrorists in *24*; I love Pink Floyd and especially the Monty Python guys when they make fun of the Bible's own stories in *Life of Brian*. I have no clever theories about all this, although I am sure God digs *Dark Side of the Moon*, or Jimmy Page's riff in "Heartbreaker," and that God giggles over irreverence (but only if it's genuinely funny).

I believe God enjoys the Beatles corpus more than I—even though Lennon puckishly (and quite accurately) declared the Beatles to be more popular than Jesus. I'm similarly sure that when I am in a funk I overhear the evocation of loneliness in "Eleanor Rigby"; or when I am in some malaise my spirit is lifted a bit by the simple optimism of "Here Comes the Sun." I continue to be moved by the gentle critique of social injustice in "Blackbird," the plaintive sorrow of "Yesterday," the sheer, giddy fun of those early covers, like "Twist and Shout" and "Rock and Roll Music." The Beatles have articulated . . . me, my world, those who have enriched, cursed, blessed, or simply populated my life. The Beatles helped me to get out what I was feeling inside. God appreciates this. You can't prove the Beatles and Pink Floyd and Monty Python and even *Family Guy* have malformed me in some dastardly, inimical way. Jesus ate with sinners and gluttons, and appears to have enjoyed himself, not sitting primly in the corner.

Carl and I practiced the Beatles a lot—and Carl was exceedingly practiced at droll, even silly humor. A master of the pun, Carl had and has a shrewd sense of irony—and no doubt he's still laughing his head off about the time he came by my girlfriend's house and stole my hubcaps. I shared my loss with him, he was gravely concerned—and then he helped me puzzle out what on earth might have transpired when the hubcaps reappeared on my car a few days later. How dense was I, not to suspect the most likely culprit? At a party ten years later, I heard him and some friends chuckling in the kitchen as he told this tale—but instead of letting him know I knew, I've planned for decades to swing by his house some night and swipe his. God loves humor; God wired us so we'd laugh, and create laughter. Sin (as Karl Barth suggested) is taking yourself too seriously; and G. K. Chesterton quaintly remarked, "Angels can fly because they can take themselves lightly."[1]

---

1. Karl Barth, *Church Dogmatics* III.4., trans. G. W. Bromiley and T. F. Torrance (Edinburgh: T.&T. Clark, 1961), 665; G.K. Chesterton, *Orthodoxy* (New York: Image, 1959), 125.

Struck from Behind

We did a thousand other silly things. In adult life, our relationship has been . . . cordial? I owe him my life in many ways, not the least of which will be the story I will tell in chapter 8 on how I managed to become a person of faith, a follower of Jesus, and a minister by vocation—no small debt! Yet we drifted, perhaps in ways that all childhood friends drift.

Our drifting had a kind of edge to it: Carl became, for lack of a better gross oversimplification, conservative, while I became liberal; I detest these labels, as I'm conservative on many things, and liberal on others. My zeal is simply to be Christian, which is neither. And yet my gratitude is no less: Carl might or might not embrace the notion of LGBT, much less Q—but was he ever called a Q? If he was my pal, he must have been.

But I had a friend, and God was there. We can be friends with people who think very differently about God, and be blessed profoundly by them. A piece of God's raucous humor is that more often than we care to admit it is someone from the other side of the theological spectrum who has been the Spirit's instrument for good in our lives.

I should increase the length of this book substantially by telling you now of the immense encouragement and companionship with which God has blessed me in the form of adult friendships: long-standing, historic friends like Randy and Tom; people I mentored who stepped up and became simple colleagues and friends, like Jason and Craig; so many coworkers in ministry, some Methodist, some not, some not even Christian; and then friends with whom there is no hint of anything spiritual: their good company and love are no less robust or pleasing to God just because God doesn't seem to come up in conversation.

The Rock Higher than I

If I think back and label instruments the Spirit used to bless me when I wasn't asking to be blessed, I am drawn to this huge rock a couple of hundred yards into the woods behind our house. When I was ten, or eleven or twelve, when I wasn't with Carl or anybody else, I could amble through the woods endlessly, just being outside, happily alone—and then I would climb on top of this huge rock. How had such a tall boulder come to be in such a place? The stone's face had mysterious indentions, and some boy from the neighborhood either made up or passed along local lore that it had been an Indian graveyard centuries ago.

So on many afternoons, I climbed up on that rock, and just sat there, doing nothing at all, not smoking or reading, but just hanging out, feeling the breeze, the sunshine's pattern dancing unpredictably through the leaves and onto my shoulders. I think the proper term to describe what I was doing would be "daydreaming." Even in those days, when children weren't as severely scheduled as today's boys and girls, daydreaming elicited scolding from teachers or parents: *You're just daydreaming, get busy, do something.* Time was for working, chores, games, something active; and so daydreaming was simply a waste of time.

As an adult, I've felt vindicated when I have read studies that reveal the ways daydreaming actually fosters creativity, emotional health, and even intelligence in children. As an adult, I wonder if we're too old to daydream—or too old not to daydream. The wonder of daydreaming, I suspect, is that you withdraw a bit from hard reality and let your mind soar—and it does soar, doesn't it? When I daydreamed on that ancient Indian rock, I never thought *Oh, I'll make a mess of my life, wind up in jail, get divorced, and become a burden to others.* Instead, the daydreamer envisions the best: marrying someone beautiful, building tall buildings, hitting the winning shot, curing cancer, and maybe even just continuing to have the freedom to do something that's nothing at all, like whiling away the hours on top of a rock. I cannot envision the childhood of Jesus without the firm conviction that he was a daydreamer, that he found some quiet spot and just—was.

God loves daydreaming, and may have been for me like a muse, dancing images in my head so I would do some longing and hoping. Theologically, we may call this Sabbath, or speak of the virtue of *solitude* versus mere loneliness. After all, on that rock I was very much alone, but I did not feel lonely. Maybe as a grownup I need to find a rock and just hang. Can aging folks still daydream?

We might question a child squandering an afternoon just squatting on an old rock; but perhaps it is a recoil of envy. When I think back to time alone on that rock, Bible verses I know commend themselves to me: "Lead me to the rock that is higher than I" (Ps 61:2); or "the Lord is my rock and my fortress" (Ps 18:2). Jesus had to have plenty to do (being the Messiah and all), but the Gospels tell us repeatedly that he "went up on a mountain by himself to pray" (Matt 14:23). But the verse I now attach in my mind to that rock is Psalm 46:10: "Be still, and know that I am God." I didn't know I was being still, or observing an unintentional Sabbath. But now I know I certainly am not being still, or not nearly often enough.

In my mid-twenties I met a man I admired immensely, and asked him one day what his secret was, how he came to be so calm, and wise. He waved off this flattery, and then told me his routine. "I get up and go to work every day" (he was a brickmason), "and then come home, do a few chores and eat dinner with Peggy. Then I go down into the basement and pull up one of those empty peach crates, and sit on it, and just think a good long while." I love that, and him, and fantasize that as I get older I'll finish a few chores and learn how to sit and think.

Chapter 4

Will You Go With Me?
Falling in Love

JESUS WAS A CHILD, then a man, in a family, with friends, even close friends. But he never married, and didn't raise children. Hebrews 4:15 assures us that Jesus was tempted in every way we are, and I can allow he had to cope with sexual allurements. But I don't think it's teetering on the edge of blasphemy to point out that Jesus never had to deal with the chronic quandaries of a marriage, or the wiles of a four-year-old in a battle of wills (or the sophomoric lunacy of an adolescent in the house). Would we know more if he'd had a few flings and a wife, or was too weary to go preach one morning after rocking a colicky baby all night? Or would the particularity of his experience slam the door shut on those whose marriages turned out differently, or weren't married at all?

For me, these relationships, with girlfriends, my wife, and my children, those that press the emotional barometer, have driven me (and you as well) to the brink of insanity, and made life a wonder well worth the bother. Where was God during those awkward days of self-discovery, when I dared to expose my most sheltered self to another whose mere word (or lack of a word) could cause me to wilt, or weep, or blush, or even stand taller by an inch or two? Did God orchestrate the quirky list of girls who captured my fancy and left a trail of mini-aches or semi-triumphs? Was God the matchmaker who hitched me forever to Lisa?

Struck from Behind

Will You Go With Me?

I am not sure when my male, romantic inner self woke up. I had always been a boy, of course; but at some point my eyes began to wander, to notice—or I should say my eyes became unable not to notice, perhaps akin to what St. Augustine imagined happened to Adam once he ate the fruit in Eden: having been able not to sin, for the rest of his life he was not able not to sin.

Not that to notice and feel stirrings deep inside is sinful. There is something lovely but unruly inside us. Anyone who says "I am master of my own existence" has never loved, has never been lured by a potential partner, has never been seized by *eros*, that pull of attraction we discover as we ramp up toward puberty, and dogs us through most of life. I recall during fifth grade staring inexplicably at the legs of a girl: her name was Linda, she wore oddly-colored fishnet hosiery. I had no clue why I kept looking at the limbs of a girl with whom I'd never had a conversation. God's quirky humor, wiring me to suffer such lowbrow enchantment.

In junior high school, these impulses flamed up more often, and more powerfully. I knew and had actually spoken with a very special girl named Nancy. Later, in high school, we would become very dear friends; but during junior high, how we might connect, or if we would connect at all, was not settled—and in retrospect, not an issue at all in *her* mind. I probably suspected as much, but could not know for sure, and needed to know. I felt much for her—and decided, for the first time, to act, to take the enormous risk of asking her to "go" with me. What that would have meant for twelve-year-olds back then is not clear—but others were coupling up and "going" together, and that seemed to be a promising resolution to the confused swirl I couldn't shut off in my gut.

So I phoned her—over and over, for many nights. I would dial the first four or five numbers, and then hang up. She was no doubt at home, minding her own business, utterly unaware both that her phone was on the verge of ringing and that a boy she knew a little could be so tortured. Finally, I got all seven numbers dialed, and I heard a ring: no backing out now. She answered. Small talk seemed impossible, so I cut to the quick. Hoping my voice wasn't trembling as much as my body (which fortunately she could not see), I took the leap: "I called to see if you would go with me." Then a pause of uncertain but agonizing duration—and then I heard her quizzical, devastating reply: "Where?"

With my soul stuck in my throat, I couldn't speak; and with what surely can't count against me as rudeness, I simply laid the phone back down on the receiver. I had not expected her to say "Yes," but I was shriven by the realization that I was totally misunderstood at the very moment of my most courageous act thus far in life. But no more misunderstood than were my own feelings that prompted the call.

I've thought about that call, and the thousand other times in life I've screwed up my courage and gotten nowhere except crushed—and wondered about God. Was God rooting for me? Sympathizing with her? Giggling? I did not pray before calling, nor repent after calling. I wonder if God wished to say "Boy, do I know how you feel!" God, constantly reaching out to us, only for God's intentions to be misconstrued, or pushed aside unwittingly. Jesus might, oddly, have hoped for Nancy's reply when he called people—and when he calls us. Jesus, with more direct intention, asks us all the time, "Will you go with me?" And he wants us, not fumbling in confusion, but with a little resolution, to ask "Where?"

These early forays into romance reveal to us the depth of humanity, our own and that of the other who isn't like us. It is that difference, yet the lure, the puzzlement, the mystery, that humbles us into realizing we don't know a fraction of what we need to know about the other, or even about what's inside our own skin. I read a poem once about a young man puzzling out his attraction to young women:

> He vaguely understood that it was not
> their flesh that was a mystery
> but something on the other side of it.[1]

What was not vague at all but pointedly clear was that I was not turning out to be the dandy girls gravitated toward, or even deigned to sit near. If I felt small when I was a child, that diminutiveness became a virtual black hole on February 29, 1968. The date is correct, as it was a Sadie Hawkins dance on Sadie Hawkins day, where roles were to be reversed: the girls were to ask the boys to dance. I'd been to a few dances, and found myself far too clammy or tongue-tied to be able to ask a girl to join me on the dance floor; but I could keep moving about, pretending to be busy, heckling others maybe, goofing with pals.

But at this dance, the boys were told to sit in chairs and wait for the girls to extend an invitation. Nowhere to hide, no trap door to slink through. Conspicuous as the unchosen, I sat rigidly, in a balled up posture. Maybe I could excuse not being asked by not looking very interested. Random giggles from people who were probably paying me no attention at all felt as if they were grenades lobbed my way.

1. Jack Gilbert, "Steel Guitars," *The Great Fires: Poems, 1982–1992* (New York: Knopf, 2004), 21.

Struck from Behind

Why did I go? Why hadn't they invented cell phones yet so I could call my dad to come rescue me? Was God sitting next to me trying to console? Was God whispering in some girl's ear, "Go ask James," but she foiled God's will by asking somebody else? Was she as paralyzed by shyness as I? The memory did provide decent sermon fodder years later when I contemplated Isaiah 65, where the prophet relates God's sad mood:

> I was ready to be sought by those who did not ask for me;
> I was ready to be found by those who did not seek me.
> I said "Here am I, here am I,"
> to a nation that did not call on my name . . .

What a great text, and I think in some measure I know how God was feeling. God wants us to be attentive to God and respond, "Here I am" (as Isaiah did back in chapter 6). Now it is God, having shown up at the Sadie Hawkins dance of my life and yours, sitting and waiting, saying "Here I am," ready to be sought and found. I've sat right next to him, unchosen.

I have also, like those who ignored me, flirted and flitted about with others, not seeking or finding the one partner who would truly be the most desirable; we get deceived by outward appearances, don't we? "He had no beauty that we should desire him; he was despised and rejected" (Isa 53:2–3), as we say on Good Friday. Yet his is the one truly lovely face, fairest Lord Jesus, disguised as the unlovely, unchosen one.

Discoveries in Going Steady

After a couple of mini-flings (and many more few failed attempts to have mini-flings), I settled in with a smart, statuesque young woman named Kay. I gave her a cheap ring, we went steady, danced at the prom, rode together to and from school, and became each other's tutors in the ways of love. These young romances help us to understand we have deep passions inside, and that our bodies are imprudent and a bit clumsy. How do I touch, and speak, and not hurt, and display care? How do I simultaneously express and yet contain my physical greed? Teachers gave us tests which were easy compared to the tests of how to make a thousand little decisions, like where to eat and which movie to see, when to go home and when to talk to another girl without arousing jealousy, why one of my friends could make me crazy by simply laughing with her in the hallway, what to say to nosy parents. Nothing equips any of us for these trials, but they prepare us for adulthood, or we hopefully can pick up the scattered debris of mistakes from the practice field and live to do better another day.

What I wonder now is how God might use these ardent yet maladroit encounters? The spiritually astute might ask about holiness, or my stewardship of my body—which rather incongruously is dubbed a "temple of the Holy Spirit" (1 Cor 6:19). God never crossed my mind as an amorous amateur. But was God furtively giving me clues about my heart and hers, wonder and beauty, the capability to hurt and be hurt, that bumbling intimacy might be our best, most surprising window into what a relationship with God might dare be like?

I was terrified my heart would be broken; even in such terror I had no clue how painful heartbreak could really be. But even if someone had explained this fact to me, I'd have loved anyhow. Why did I choose Kay? I'm not sure I ever thought it through. She was pretty, and bright, with a sense of humor. She had a big advantage over other girls: she seemed to be interested in me. But at the end of the day, she was like lots of girls, just as I was like lots of boys. We just came together. Love's impulsivity is reason enough, I suppose.

Certainly there must be some taming, some discipline of our irrational desires, or else we could never be holy for a moment, or stay married, or out of jail. But those cravings, that "zoo of lusts, a bedlam of ambitions" (as C. S. Lewis put it[2]) inside me? God put all that in me, perhaps as a test, perhaps to make things fun, perhaps so I might procreate, perhaps as a foretaste of the even more intense pleasure that will be our life in heaven joining the angels in songs of praise.

For me, too many of these forays into romance ended shabbily. How could it be that a pretty, sweet, and entirely innocent young woman could inflict real physical pain upon me with her kind words, "I just don't see us having a future as a couple"? How would I have inflicted pain, since I'd never ranked my charms high enough to think losing them might be a problem? And why did my awkward flops come back to haunt me later? One woman, twenty-five years after the fact, sat me down and gave me a stern lecture regarding how I'd hurt her. I could only apologize and explain how utterly inept and clueless I was back in the day (and continue to be today). Perhaps it is from such muddles that we learn that unwelcome wrinkle in the fabric of forgiveness: we may be forgiven by God or ourselves, or even wrest forgiveness from others, but there are still consequences that linger out there and in here, and we need more mercy than we'd imagined.

2. C. S. Lewis, *Surprised by Joy: The Shape of My Early Life* (San Diego: Harvest, 1955), 226.

Struck from Behind

Of course, my own parents somehow managed to endure a disastrous marriage for more than twenty years, and then it finally ended shabbily. Did their marital combat, or the absence of tenderness, cause me to hold back? I don't recall even one moment's trepidation that I would mimic the mess their marriage was; if anything I swore I'd reverse any lingering curse and create total marital bliss—a determination that hasn't done my own marriage much good.

Then I think of the most revealing words ever spoken to me, uttered by my father during the one and only conversation we ever had about his failed marriage to my mother. Striving to pull the lid off old secrets, I asked why he had stayed with her for so many years. I assumed the answer was something like "You just didn't get divorced in those days," or "We stayed together so you kids could have a home," or "I kept hoping things might get better." His answer, so obvious, so lovely, and so dumbfounding, had never once occurred to me. A bit puzzled by my inquiry, "Why did you stay with her?" he replied with thinly guarded pathos: "It was because I loved her."

Do You Love Me?

After years of hits and misses, I settled in to being single and feeling pretty much okay with it. I had already been a full-time pastor for four years, and despite frenetic, constant efforts by my parishioners to get me married, I was approaching thirty, and still very much a bachelor.

One elderly woman, Boots Wagoner, as she would exit worship each week, reached up, pulled my head toward hers, kissed me on the lips, and said, "If you just get married you'll be a great preacher." On many Sundays, some young woman whose name I did not know would be sitting down front, a niece or coworker or neighbor someone had brought in hopes of sparking some mutual interest. My dear parishioners loved me—but was it that they wanted me married so much as they felt uncomfortable with the prickly issues involved in a pastor engaged in something so dicey as dating?

And so they escorted young women who seemed to fit the part—or were of age and had a pulse—but I frustrated their designs. Instead of singing "Matchmaker matchmaker, make me a match," I'd come to murmur under my breath, "Matchmaker, matchmaker, please leave me alone."

My friend Reverend Ron Hall did not. He devised some clever ruse for me to meet Lisa after a class I was teaching at Myers Park United Methodist Church, where her father had been pastor, where we would eventually marry, and where I would serve as pastor for many years. We met, drifted out to the parking lot, and chatted a long time; that we now recall as Date #1. Things progressed, more rapidly than I'd thought possible. Extravagant, over the top ideas floated through my head—and it struck me that love, the kind you have to own and proclaim, and ask for in return, was an irresistible force that needed some resolution, a declaration, a cementing.

So the big night finally arrived. I put on my best domestic front and prepared a candlelight dinner of chicken and stuffed mushrooms. We ate, and then I serenaded her at the piano. I cannot be sure, but I suspect that the entire membership of my church had circled the parsonage in a prayer vigil, so determined were they for a match to occur.

Finally, I took my life in my hands and declared to her as firmly yet tenderly as possible: "I love you." No cuisine, no serenading could guarantee what her reply might be. She could have squirmed and muttered, "Uh, well, you're a nice guy, but . . ." Instead she gently embraced my trembling self, nodded, and said, "I love you too." With only a couple of minor detours, things rushed forward; we were married within the year, and pregnant not long after.

I have thought a lot about that lovely, perilous moment when I said, "I love you," and what I can thus recall about God. I'm not sure I'd say God was the secret matchmaker, and I know God didn't make her say Yes. You can't force love—and I think that is the revelation. The beauty of that moment resides not merely in the happy conclusion to the story. The beauty of the moment—and we have all been there in some way or another—emerges out of the utter vulnerability of the lover, for beauty teeters on the edge of darkness. When you tell someone "I love you," you forsake all control, you abandon self-protection. You take this marvelous, fragile crystal of your self, and you hand it to another person, who might drop you to the floor, and you watch your self being shattered into pieces that can never quite be glued back together. Or, the beloved might cradle your wholly risked self to her breast.

And something we forget in the midst of virtually every beautiful moment: when we celebrate a newfound love, when we utter and absorb words that matter and thus the world changes, some door slams shut behind you. Dizzy with what is transpiring before you, you may not hear the door slam, but later you realize that something got foreclosed on you.

Struck from Behind

Love's Lies

Wasn't what I tried that evening a reenactment of the events of Holy Week, and the whole purpose, frustration, and then fulfillment of the Incarnation of our Lord? Jesus came to us, and loved us. He prepared a meal, and then offered the fragile crystal of his own perfect, holy, beautiful self to us. His very existence, his way of being, his words, his healing, his courting of danger, his offering up of his very life on the cross was God saying "I love you—do you love me?"

Our immense regret is that instead of taking the crystal wonder of the divine self, which would be our very own blessed life, we hesitate, we prevaricate, we think back to some old relationship or diversion and aren't ready to foreclose. And so we let the gift of God's own self slip through our fingers. Christ was shattered—and is repeatedly shattered by our inexplicable inability to seize (or be seized by) the only precious gift that really matters. And so we spend our lives (hopefully) staring at the broken pieces, the crucified body of our Lord, and we ask forgiveness, for a fresh opportunity to say Yes.

My daily project during those early weeks of our courtship would be well-described in what has proven to be my favorite book about marriage, *As For Me and My House*. Walter Wangerin, narrating his wooing of Thanne, exposed what I would not have admitted to myself at the time:

> Love lies a little. Love edits the facts in order to continue to feel good. Love allows me an innocent misperception of my fiancée, while it encourages in her a favorable misperception of myself . . . I put my best foot forward. Was I deceiving her? Of course not. I was showing her what I truly believed myself to be in the generous light of her love—and what I knew I could become, if only for the prize of her hand in marriage.[3]

Here I suspect God truly is watching closely, smiling, and cheering us on, hoping the misperception becomes reality. If it takes erotic urgings for us to begin to dream of being our best conceivable self, God must be pleased. God might even brag that God made us this way with this very purpose in mind. Then I also wonder if God doesn't sigh a bit, and wish that when in worship, or in life, we might approach the throne of grace with our best foot forward, living into what we truly believe we might be in the generous light of God's love, what we know we just might become if only for the

---

3. Walter Wangerin, *As For Me and My House: Crafting Your Marriage to Last* (Nashville: Thomas Nelson, 1990), 31, 33.

36

prize of God's intimate fellowship—which we have already won, or which has been won for us.

I have to admit to a lower than average sense of God as a matchmaker who brings someone into your life and, Cupid-like, prods or even irresistibly melds two lives. But I can easily conjure up an image of the goodness of God, and it is in the face of Lisa, the woman who chose me, who's stayed with me, reared children with me, and served God in noble, selfless ways. What good fortune: to have someone who is always 100 percent behind me, even if I am wrong, and shows me every day what grace looks like, and how God feels in God's own heart by sticking with me, and tenderly caring for me, and welcoming an echo of that love in return.

A Flock of Goats on the Slopes of Gilead

Allow me a little aside on a book of the Bible that has helped me think about things erotic. As a relatively normal adolescent and young adult who thought a lot about sex (and not at all by choice), it was of considerable comfort when, in my first serious study of the entire Bible, I stumbled across the elegant, erotic love poetry that is the Song of Songs. My friends and I reaped much humor from its pages, advising one another to use its "pickup" lines: "Your eyes are doves, your hair is like a flock of goats on the slopes of Gilead; your cheeks are like halves of a pomegranate, your neck like the tower of David . . ." How good of God to tuck into the pages of scripture an entire book that articulates the strongest feelings and most palpable intimacies we experience in this life. If the Bible can talk about it, maybe we can. If our tradition, which contemplates the intersection

37

of God and human life, was intrigued enough by sexuality to stamp the Song of Songs as scriptural, then perhaps we can discover the intersection between the divine and our most intimate selves.

On Tuesday mornings in the Fall of 1979, three of us who were Old Testament PhD candidates sat around a table with Father Roland Murphy and read the Song of Songs slowly, and in Hebrew. Our wise teacher was in the early stages of writing a commentary on the Song. We labored at translation, and compared Egyptian and Cuneiform love poetry. Being an all-male group, we blushed at times (and shared a few laughs) over the Song's eroticism.

Murphy was adamant about the unmistakable difference between this ancient eroticism and what passes for sexy today. It is not merely that the language is more eloquent, the passions expressed less trivialized. What is striking is that, for all its supple imagery that makes you sigh or blush, there is no graphic consummation of things, no immediate grinding in the sack. The language is all about desire and searching, not finding and having; these lovers long for one another, catch a glimpse, seek, miss each other, yearn.

Romance: less about possession, grabbing and climax, and more about pursuit, absence, and yearning? Shakespeare wrote history's most romantic adventure, and in his most unforgettable scene, Romeo is planted squarely on *terra firma*, while Juliet is perched high up, leaning over her balcony. He magnificently praises her beauty, she expresses her penchant for him—and then he returns home, and she goes back to bed, alone. In modern stories, they don't bother with the poetic praising; Romeo simply climbs the trellis and they jump into the sack.

"Parting" really "is such sweet sorrow." The waiting is precisely the most powerful passion. Love grows not by proximity but over some distance, and time. This is a theological memoir, so there is no time to explore this in depth, but I wonder if my children, or anybody much in our culture, will ever comprehend this more robust, titillating ethic of physical intimacy. Everything now is about consummation, nobody waits, crude images abound. Perhaps more tragically, this manner of seeking, longing, and waiting is a mirror of what our relationship with God could be like, but not when we think of God as an object to be possessed, and right now. God fashioned the hollowness inside us, not as an evil to be cured, but as the most marvelous of all gifts. The nagging hankering we feel inside is God's voice, calling us home, keeping us a bit restless so we will forever seek after God.

Permission to Marry—and a Blessing

Among our many treasured photographs, one stands out. My wife's grand-mother, Mrs. Stevens (we never called her Grace, but always Mrs. Stevens), the matriarch of the rather large clan into which I had married nine years earlier, was dying. Back when we'd decided to marry, Lisa and I merely informed her parents of our engagement. But I knew I had to ask permission from Mrs. Stevens. On a knee, I had made my request, and she was pleased enough to grab my face in both hands and kiss me on the lips. Then, quoting scripture as only the wife of a Baptist preacher could do, she raised a hand toward Lisa and said "From now on, you will decrease, and he will increase." We nodded, but then laughed out loud when we drove away, for she was a woman who had never done much of that decreasing.

Back to her dying, and the photograph. For ninety-five years she lived independently and enjoyed good health and sound mind. Yet in her final days she became confused, a tad belligerent, regrettably difficult, and we had little choice but to place her in the skilled care facility at Arbor Acres in Winston-Salem. About this time, our third child, Noah, was born. We had expected a third girl; among the nine grandchildren in my wife's immediate family, poor Noah was the only boy. Grandmother Stevens had known my girls, stitched gifts for them, posed for photos with them sitting in her lap. But now she was in dire straits in a nursing home.

We decided to take Noah for a visit anyhow. Even though we expected to be with her only a few moments, it just seemed the right thing to do. Instead of what sadly had become usual for her, being bedridden, mixed up, and combative, when we entered the room with a baby, her eyes flew open, she raised up in the bed, smiled, and asked, "Who is this?" We

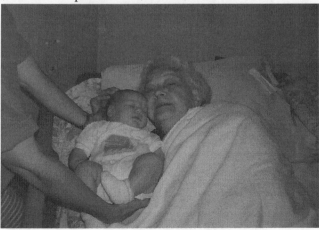

said, "This is Noah, our new son, your great grandson." She extended her frail arms, embracing him as Lisa placed him next to her on the bed. Then she kissed him on the head, and said "Bless you."

He was blessed. I suspect Mrs. Stevens was blessed. I know Lisa and I in our marriage were much blessed by this moment, as the one who gave us permission to marry and knew God so well blessed our family with the laying on of hands once more.

Do such blessings matter? Are they merely cute, sweet sentiments? Or were the Bible's authors on to something when they reported that the elderly channeled some holy power into those on whom they laid hands and spoke? Joseph brought his twin sons to his father Jacob on his death-bed. When he saw them he asked, "Who are these?" Joseph said to his father, "They are my sons, whom God has given me here." And he said, "Bring them to me, I pray you, that I may bless them" (Gen 48:8–9). Jacob's eyes "were dim with age, so that he could not see"—but he kissed and embraced them. He stretched out his hands and blessed them.

Shortly after Jesus was born, Mary and Joseph took him to the temple. A wizened, devout man named Simeon, "inspired by the Spirit . . . took him up in his arms and blessed him" (Luke 2:27–28). His bless-ing certainly wasn't for long life for the boy or riches and happiness for his parents. Jesus was set for a holy destiny, one that would "pierce" his mother's heart (Luke 2:35). Lisa and I have certainly been blessed beyond measure, and our hearts have been pierced just as surely, as the story of the children will show.

Chapter 5

The Children
Sarah, Grace, Noah

ALL CHILDREN BREAK THEIR parents' hearts—and only because they are
the shimmering delight of their parents' hearts. Somehow I did not pay the
slightest heed to the inevitable time when my children would no longer
live with me and be the focal point of each day's activity. That is, until my
oldest went off for six weeks to Governor's School, a pretty chic summer
program for gifted kids. Exactly one year from the summer Sarah would
leave for college, and I began to realize this was a trial run of sorts—not for
her, she'd do just fine, but for me.

Love Proved in the Letting Go

We piled her stuff in the car, drove to Winston-Salem, unloaded, met other
kids and parents—and then we were whisked off, without our children,
to an auditorium where some Governor's School official seemed to know
precisely what was swirling in my head. She made a little speech about
leaving, trusting, letting go. My emotions got the better of me—and while
I did not jot down her precise remarks, I shall never forget that she recited
a poem by Cecil Day-Lewis, the Irish poet laureate and father of the acclaimed actor Daniel Day-Lewis.

> It is eighteen years ago . . . I watched you play
> . . . then, like a satellite
> wrenched from its orbit, go drifting away.
> That hesitant figure, eddying away

like a winged seed loosened from its parent stem . . .
I have had worse partings, but none that so
gnaws at my mind still. Perhaps it is roughly
saying what God alone could perfectly show—
how selfhood begins with a walking away,
and love proved in the letting go.

That cut me deeply. I walked away from Salem College, and one year later I deposited Sarah at Duke University. I kept it together in her presence, but as I walked out of the dorm I nearly collapsed. I couldn't get air into my lungs. My legs felt like jelly supported by flimsy sticks. Somehow we made it back to the car and drove away. Maudlin, yes, although Day-Lewis's word, "wrenched," is the most fitting adjective for that awful day.

This letting go: I had been so determined to do things for my children, not to control them but to be sure they were cared for, loved, provided for—no doubt because I didn't get what I needed when I was an adolescent and swore a sacred oath that things would be different for my children. My greatest pleasure was running some simple errand to help them out, to take them to the doctor, to play Chutes & Ladders endlessly on the floor, to watch *Beauty and the Beast* (again, and again), to get them to piano lessons or softball practice. I wish someone had told me, before I got started on all this heroic parenting, what Jean Vanier wrote about love, words I didn't stumble upon until my kids were mostly grown, and I had proven myself not gifted at letting go:

> To love someone is not to do things *for* them, but to reveal to them their beauty and value, to say "You are beautiful. You are important. I trust you. You can trust yourself." We all know well that we can do things for others and in the process crush them, making them feel that they are incapable of doing things by themselves. To love someone is to reveal to them the light that is shining in them.[1]

As a dad, I made plenty of mistakes, most of them either trying too hard, or a determination not to make the mistakes my own parents made—but my children were loved. I had to laugh out loud when the dad in Pat Conroy's *The Prince of Tides* tells his three children,

> "I know we're screwing you up a little bit every day. If we knew how we were doing it, we'd stop. We wouldn't do it ever again, because we adore you. But we're parents and we can't help it. It's

1. Jean Vanier, *From Brokenness to Community* (New York: Paulist, 1992), 16.

our job to screw you up. Do you understand?" "No," they agreed
in a simultaneous chorus.[2]

I have some regrets, and can only hope they are misplaced. I wish we had
gotten into hiking, fishing, camping or some such—but I'm not a hiker or
fisherman; I'm a writer, a talker. I wish we'd had more fun, but how exactly
would you go about raising the fun quotient? And we did have much fun.

I wish I had been less anxious. Sadly for me, and more sadly for my
children, I underlined (and then circled) Joan Didion's remark about her
daughter Quintana: "Once she was born I was never not afraid."[3] But it really *is* dangerous out there—and what if something happened? I wish we'd
been more devout, maybe reading Psalms at night. Nobody gets this stuff
right; George Eliot told the truth when she wrote "Perhaps nothing 'ud be
a lesson to us if it didn't come too late."[4]

But it is never too late to remember. So there is much love, and many
stories, and I certainly wish I'd written more down. And I have to wonder
what it will cost me to tell what I recall: the family deal always has been
that if I mention one of my kids in a sermon, he or she gets $5—not to
mention my ironclad commitment never to say anything that might verge
on embarrassing.

2. Pat Conroy, *The Prince of Tides* (New York: Bantam, 1986), 15.
3. Joan Didion, *Blue Nights* (New York: Knopf, 2011), 54.
4. George Eliot, *Adam Bede* (New York: Signet, 1961), 198.

Thousands of Little Things

So now their childhoods, which I wished would never end, are all memory, captured in my mind, in photos, a few videos, stories they might tell after I'm gone, hopefully to their own children. We would pile in the car and listen to the inimitable Sugar Beats, a band that produced kiddie covers of pop songs I'd loved as a kid: "Big Yellow Taxi," "Lean on Me," and "Put a Little Love in Your Heart." We drove to Sea World, got splashed by Shamu, and then when it was time to leave could not locate our car—in the pouring rain. We flew to Paris and ate TexMex—two nights in a row!—and then when we finally dined in an elegant French restaurant, Sarah ordered lobster, only to break down in tears pleading not to have lobster after they brought the poor creature to her at the table—alive.

What do the kids remember from trips to grand historical and scenic locations? The dog that barked incessantly in the square of Honfleur, and the random whiffle ball game on the lawn in the Cotswolds. We drove all over the western United States, and the girls poked fun at Noah, young enough to be perched in a child car seat, for singing along with Shania Twain's "Man! I feel like a woman." It's always a little thing: on Christmas morning, Grace, aged four, gave everyone a dollar—which was the sum total of her life savings.

Lest you get the wrong idea about her, not long afterward we were down the street with friends. Grace climbed into their little tree house, hoisting a cinder block behind her; she waited patiently until her sister walked under the tree, and then dropped the block on her head. Noah and I drove all over the country trying out and ranking various roller coasters; Cedar Point's Millennium still wins the day. Sarah and I harmonized to Raffi, Noah and I devised a jig, jag then explosion handshake, and Grace and I munched M&Ms in the dark after her bedtime story.

What is intriguing to me about these memories is that they are utterly common, *and* entirely unique. No one reading this recalls a little boy singing "Man! I feel like a woman" near Canyon de Chelly or eating TexMex in St. Germain. And yet you can recall something analogous. This is our common life: each of us utterly unique, with shared bonds of mortality, dreams, brokenness, loves, losses and surprises—and a good God who is there, the way Johner the robin was always there. When Sarah was three or four, she spotted a robin in the yard and dubbed him (her?) Johner. Wherever we would drive, across town or four states away, she would take a gander out the car window and holler, "Look, daddy! It's Johner!" I should have thought to tell her God is like Johner, or the whole holy flock of Johners together, always nearby, never controlling our route or activities, but there, pleased to be noticed, and to elicit some joy in the recognition.

I try to imagine what it must be like in God's heart to have the privilege of spending all these moments with families. God knows the secrets, the perplexities, the little interchanges that mercifully remain private, and also the little delights, a chuckle, a cookie sneaked, an adolescent gambol unseen by mom or dad, a tender pat on the back.

Although other parents had warned us, Lisa and I were baffled by how very different one child could be from another. Sarah and Grace: was somebody swapped in the hospital? Can they share a shred of genetic or psychological material? And then Noah arrives: would he be like thing one or thing two? . . . and the answer was Neither. Yet a third quite bewildering and captivating being, a Howell but oddly mutated. How are they kin?

And if three can confound me, what must it be like for God, who has to keep up with not three but three hundred million in America and a few billion more around the globe—and that's just right now. God remembers all the others gone before; and if God transcends time, God can right now remember those not yet born. And God knows the hidden complexities in them all, including my own children who elude me, try as I might to know them as thoroughly as possible. God could have saved God's self an unfathomable expenditure of trouble by stamping us out as little identical toy soldiers. But God did the snowflake thing, the fingerprint thing, the DNA thing, and we are all wildly peculiar, inherently mysterious, and because of this, alluringly lovable.

Somewhere Over the Rainbow

But then the love may or may not happen; the treasure may or may not punch its way through to the heart. If it happens you're a lucky dog. If not—well, there's work to be done, and a church is required. When Sarah was just four years old, she entered our church talent show and took second place—quite unjustly I might add, losing out to a family of dancing squirrels. I accompanied her on the piano as she sang "Somewhere Over the Rainbow," sitting on the piano, cabaret style. With no bias, I can tell you Judy Garland never sang it better.

Struck from Behind

After the last note, the audience erupted in applause. We took a bow, then hurried side-stage where I swooped her up, twirled her around, hugged and kissed her, and said, "Oh Sarah, I love you." One of my church members was standing right there—and she said to me, "I wish my father had done that." A little slow to catch on, I said, "You wish your father had played the piano?" She said, "No, I wish my father had loved me."

I can't fashion a properly nuanced psychological explanation of this, but lots of people are like me: their relationship with "dad" is a struggle. Dad wasn't there, or was there but not really there. This nagging upset riddles us long after we're grown, long after dad is buried and in the grave. And we look for substitutes, father-figures, teachers, coaches, bosses, spouses—desperately seeking that blessing, that affirmation, something to fill that gap inside. Jesus' best known story is his best known for a reason: a father gazed down that road, hoping against hope, until the boy walked home, and the father scooped him up and threw an unforgettable party.

Jesus knew we'd need that story. His words (nothing but words, just an old, made-up story!) actually heal, and fill that gray hollow place where dad should have been, or even tried to be. God was offstage at that talent show when I twirled Sarah—and my words unwittingly resounded as an echo of the love we can't stop yearning for, waking up a chilly memory in my friend, and frankly in my own self. Yet at the same time, that echo became the music of some angel teasing us with the proleptic presence of what will one day be our most potent memory—of a place over the rainbow, a land we heard of in a lullaby, where dreams come true, the dream of love and belonging that God causes to dance in all of our heads by night, and by day.

My friend's father may well have loved her. There is some fracture at the core of human existence, isn't there? As intense as my love for those I love feels to me, I realize they might not get it, or it might not prove to be a healing balm. Especially at that letting go point, the risk expands and might just overwhelm. If the plan is to craft a life so your children might be Christian, the peril mounts, given the wider not-so-Christian culture which is the very air our children breathe.

High Risk

It's all so risky—and the circumstances of Sarah's birth underlined that for me, and quite humorously. Lisa and I had gone for the little tour of the birthing areas at Presbyterian Hospital. Our guide boasted of the homey comforts and clinical quality of the labor and delivery rooms. I raised my hand, prompting Lisa to jab me in the side (as I'd embarrassed her a few other times during this process of Lamaze classes and OB/GYN visits). "What if the labor and delivery rooms are full?" Our guide soothingly assured me, "They are never full."

Since I'm bothering to tell this, you can see where we're heading. Before dawn on April 2, 1987, Lisa woke me so I could time her contractions. *Two minutes apart? We're supposed to be at the hospital already!* I drove madly through the dark, and pulled up at the appropriate entrance. A woman helped Lisa into a wheelchair and instructed me to go park the car over there someplace.

After doing so, I jogged through the door myself, and asked "Where is Lisa Howell?" That same woman pointed and said, "In the high risk area." They nearly had to put me on a gurney to push me to the cardiac arrest area . . . but of course, Lisa was in "high risk" because, yes indeed, the labor and delivery rooms were full. A little fist pump of triumph!—and relief, then a swift realization that I'd best keep my trivial victory to myself.

When Sarah finally did emerge a few hours later via C-section, there was high risk indeed: a crowd of people in medical garb began rushing about and looked more concerned than I thought they should, although I couldn't know if this were normal or not. Turns out Sarah was under some duress. After a few hours she was fine, but the high risk of simply being (for her) and loving (for us) was begun.

Grace similarly couldn't be pushed out and had to be removed by C-section. We'd agreed on the name Abigail, but after Dr. Vandiver announced "It's a girl," Lisa looked up and asked, "Can we name her Grace?" In no position to argue, I acceded, and she has been Grace, has required grace, and has taught us more than we ever wanted to know about the true meaning of grace.

With Noah, we scheduled that third C-section. Dr. Clay Harrell hoisted him out of Lisa, held him up full frontal in my face, and said, "Dad, is it a girl or a boy?" All I could muster was "You're the MD—can't you tell?" I must say I was rather startled in the late twentieth century to see the giddy pride among the nurses when he turned out to be a *he*; "Ah, dad, you got a boy, I know you always wanted a boy!"

I wonder what Jesus' birth was like. I love the glowing chiaroscuro of Rembrandt's "Adoration of the Shepherds," but I should imagine that back then, whether you were in a manger or in a palace, considerable trepidation was the dominant mood during labor and immediately afterward. Onlookers would do what they could, but they must have shuddered over the loss of blood, with no antibiotics or pain relievers, no suctioning of the infant's lungs, no warming lamps or physician's expertise. When Jesus was born, Mary must have been relieved she'd survived—and then had to endure that agonizing wait of however many seconds before his first cry. Mary heard Jesus' first cry, which Madeleine L'Engle suggested might have sounded "like a bell."[5] She held him to her breast, her worst fears allayed, certainly anxious, voicing a prayer of gratitude, wondering how they would make it through the night.

God thought: I want them to know me—so I will do *this*. I will be born, just as all of them were born, with the high risk, the inarticulate cry, the tender embrace. Much patience and love would be required, and given. The hospital where Sarah was born plays a little lullaby on the loud speaker throughout the hospital when a child is born. I suspect the angels sing some chorus for God to hear each time a child is born in a cozy place like a hospital or in a hut in a jungle, and God recalls Mary's agony, and joy, and the sound of Jesus' first cry, and God smiles, again and again.

Behaving Like People

When we first had children, somebody loaned me and Lisa a videotape of that old Bill Cosby routine on parenting, how he and his wife "used

5. Madeleine L'Engle, *A Cry Like a Bell* (Wheaton, IL: Shaw, 2000), 55.

to be intellectuals" before they had children. We laughed more than was warranted, to the point of tears. The humbling that is parenthood is hopeful spiritually, and tears are cleansing—although you don't realize it when you're in the midst of the humbling, or when you're reduced to crying.

I think I wanted things to go smoothly, which of course they never do. I think that, in our home, I harbored in my mind (not openly, and never acknowledging this) a preconceived story I wished would unfold, instead of discovering the story that was actually unfolding. That's my sin in parenting; I wish I could catch a mulligan on that, but it's done, and in retrospect I hope and pray God was patient with me, and will do the Genesis 50:20 and Romans 8:28 things and bring good out of it all.

I was feeling forlorn during an awkward month when my oldest was shutting me out from her inner self, when my middle child was just plain getting on my nerves, and when my youngest was proving to be stubbornly resistant to and downright resentful of my counsel, when I stumbled upon a thought from Russell Baker. As his children waded through adolescence, he was dismayed to realize that "the values I'd been bred to cherish and live by were now held in contempt." He found it hard "to speak with them as a father ought to speak to his children." When he attempted counsel or correction, the response was "a great deal of invisible but nevertheless palpable sneering."

> Adolescence was finishing its nasty work of turning them from dear sweet children into the same ornery people you meet every day as you go through life. The kind of people who insist on disagreeing with you. And behaving like people.[6]

Reading saves me once more: "And behaving like people." Mine really have never sneered too much, and generally wait patiently for me to stop talking when I speak as a father should speak. I think I am grateful—for their patience, and even more that they really are people.

Pluck is good. Grace got more of it than my other two put together. One evening, when Grace was maybe seven, I heard this dialogue out in the hallway. Lisa: "Grace, brush your teeth." Grace: "I already did." Lisa: "No you didn't." Grace: "How do you know?" Lisa: "Your toothbrush is dry." Grace: "That's because I dried it." Lisa (frustration rising): "Why did you dry it?" Grace (matter of factly): "If you don't dry it, the wet stuff dribbles down and forms yucky stuff." Lisa insisted she come and brush

6. Russell Baker, "Life with Mother," *Inventing the Truth: The Art and Craft of Memoir*, ed. William Zinsser (Boston: Houghton-Mifflin), 29–30.

her teeth. But in my view, if you're clever enough to devise such a ploy, you get a pass on the toothbrushing.

God admires pluck. All those quirky Bible stories that make rule-breakers uncomfortable tell us something about God's appreciation of the wiles of the crafty. Think of Tamar getting dolled up to seduce her father-in-law Judah (Gen 38), or that dishonest steward in Jesus' parable (Luke 16), or the Syrophoenician woman's counter to Jesus dissing her, "Even the dogs under the table eat the children's crumbs" (Mark 7:28)—and even Jesus cheekily refusing to cower before Pilate and Herod, using their violent paranoia for his holy purposes.

I thought if my children depended on me they would be blessed—although the beauty in them is their autonomy, which is not entirely inconsistent with dependence upon God. Grace again was the most ferociously independent, preferring to do it her own way, even if she were wrong, even if consequences would prompt any other mortal to act differently. I think of the first fender benders for my children, and all were perfectly in character. Sarah phoned me in tears, terribly upset she'd damaged the car and somebody else's; but on further investigation, she had tapped somebody in a parking lot, the sum total of the damage being a cracked turn signal. Noah backed into a parked car; regrettably for me he was probably right when he immediately claimed he would never have done so if I hadn't been sitting in the car making him nervous.

But Grace: instead of making a little dent, she crashed into a friend's car and caused about $7000 in damages. That was at about 10:45 a.m., but I didn't learn about it until mid-afternoon, when my cell phone rang and I heard her ask, "Dad, can I borrow your car?" "And why would you need to borrow my car?" "I wrecked mine." At age sixteen, she had gotten it towed, dealt with the police, caught a ride home, never breaking a sweat, clearly having missed out on the rule of the universe for adolescents: when you wreck you car, you phone dad immediately, and emotionally.

Those who think God manipulates everything are clearly misguided; and even those who imagine that God wants a weak-kneed obsequious dependence upon God might be missing something too. God makes us for freedom, not to go do as we wish, but to stand on our feet, with some dignity, exercising the capabilities God wired us with, to go and be out there.

Sometimes a gritty independence is tough on a parent, and at many junctures it must be even more agonizing for God. I think of the poignant scene near the end of the film version of Norman Maclean's *A River Runs Through It*. This father, a pastor like me, had two sons, one straight and reliably good, the other wild, tiptoeing along the edge of disaster until he lost his life. Unlike Jesus' story of the prodigal son, in Maclean's story the wayward son is irrevocably lost. The father spoke little of the son he lost until, in his last sermon before his own death, he said,

> Each one of us here today will, at one time in our lives, look upon a loved one in need and ask the same question: We are willing Lord, but what, if anything, is needed? For it is true that we can seldom help those closest to us. Either we don't know what part of ourselves to give, or more often than not, that part we have to give . . . is not wanted. And so it is those we live with and should know who elude us . . . But we can still love them . . . We can love—completely—even without complete understanding.[7]

I am fairly certain God feels this way with us: God loves, but doesn't seem to be able to help, or the help God offers isn't wanted, or perhaps even needed. And then we do the same with the Lord: we love the Lord, we want to help the Lord, but we are a bit unsure what part of ourselves to give to the Lord. But we love. We may not understand.

I Have Been Changed for Good

Perhaps we are the ones helped by the loving. Can we safely assume God is helped by loving us too? Here is one of my loveliest memories, a lucky coincidence really, and corny in a happy way. When my daughters were exiting high school, they were graced with some fortunate timing on Broadway: *Wicked*, the terrific story of the witches from the Wizard of Oz back in their high school days, was touring, and wildly popular. The musical's most triumphant song is one whose words articulated not only what my girls were feeling about friends and that emergence into adulthood, but also what I was feeling about them, and what I will always feel: "Because I knew you, I have been changed for good." When I love, I am the beneficiary. If God is like us, or if we are like God, then perhaps God too is enriched by loving us.

I think my hesitancy in letting go hasn't been about clinging to a big, eighteen-year-old person. I think I just loved those early years so much. I can't imagine any dad ever delighting more than I did in that ever-lengthening laundry list of things parents get to do with children: pushing

7 The film combines two different moments from the book for this scene: Norman Maclean, *A River Runs Through It and Other Stories* (New York: Pocket, 1976), 89 and 113.

51

the swing, playing catch, nightly reading, driving to practices, grabbing an ice cream cone . . . I get choked up just typing the list, so I'd best stop with hide and seek. Grace was the runaway champion, capable of curling herself up inside places no one would dream of looking; and Noah was a dud—a fun dud, as he enjoyed hiding so much he could not refrain from giggling out loud.

I giggle, shudder, stammer, and try to find words to share the depth of love I've had for Sarah, Grace, and Noah. How could they know? I've tried to tell, and show, but then I've had to do all that parenting which might look like a harder caricature of the inner regard and overflow of emotion. And I've had my own issues which cloud things—but then we love in flawedness and brokenness, or not at all. If I start typing and try to express how much or in how many ways I love them, this memoir would run through a dozen or more sequels.

Most likely they will never fully comprehend the glory, ache and wonder of this love. I suppose they may get a little glimpse if they have their own children, although the thunderstorm and gentle breeze of emotion will be their own in that case. The gift finally is in the loving: how good it is to love. Probably I have never been more like God, and thus never closer to God, than in loving, however awkwardly, my children, and wife.

The End

And how will it all end? We cannot know; as of this writing I am trying to sort through how to become a parent of the big people who are professionals, spouses, and parents themselves. And if our narrative plays out the way so many do, at some point those big children will be required to treat me as something of the child, as my needs mount, and my mobility and mental capabilities diminish.

I think how much of the parent-child relationship, in its happiest and saddest guises, transpires by the side of or on a bed. Children are tucked into bed, read to in bed, nursed back to health in a bed; a clap of thunder scuttles the kids into the parents' bed. Noah was not a good sleeper, waking up and invading our room long before Lisa and I were ready to get up and face a still-dark morning. Once he got to her side of the bed and said, "Mom." Before she could rise from her slumber, I said, "You stay in bed; I'll get up with him today." But he pointed a little finger at me and said, "No, Daddy, you stay in bed. Mom gets to get up with me today. You get to get up with me tomorrow!"—as if it were some sort of privilege to have your sleep interrupted.

And, of course, it was a privilege, and I'd give a month's sleep now to go back and relive that single morning. The day may well come when I am the one in the bed, and he comes to me again, to say words of love, or to kneel and say a prayer, or even—impossible as it seems, given the richness of this good life—to say goodbye.

In the Gospels we read a little about Joseph—but only a little. Joseph is in the Christmas pageants, always, but he never has any lines, or actions. He just holds the donkey's reins and gazes—not a bad role at all, this simple privilege of being near Jesus. We think of Joseph the carpenter, apprenticing Jesus in his shop. But by the time Jesus strides onto the world stage as an adult, Joseph is never mentioned again, although we do hear about Jesus' mother. Joseph must have died sometime after Jesus was twelve, but before he was in his mid-twenties.

How did he die? In backwater Nazareth in the first century, you died at home. Surely Mary and Jesus were there, by his bedside. I picture Jesus holding his father's hand, wiping his brow, saying those words that need to be said at such times, and lifting his eyes in prayer. When Joseph breathed his last, Jesus saw. He shed tears, and kissed him goodbye. Like any parent, I hope it will be so when my hour comes. But even if the kids or Lisa can't get there, if my loves aren't by the bed or whatever sad place I happen to be when I leave this good earth, I have come to a pretty firm conviction that I won't really be alone after all.

Chapter 6

Hospital Visitations
Why Have You Forsaken Me?

A FEW YEARS AGO, I was part of a training session for non-ordained people who'd signed up to make hospital visits. An icebreaker question was posed: "When you walk into a hospital, how do you feel?" Various "lite" answers were offered, and then a tall, quiet young man, when his turn came, paused, appeared to plunge into some unfathomable abyss of thought, and finally said, "When I walk into a hospital, my palms sweat, and my feet hurt." He never said why. It could be he had at some point left behind some immeasurably valuable treasure of a life inside one. Or perhaps he'd only been in a hospital once or twice, for nothing of consequence, but the sheer specter of this perilous front line of the battle zone against inevitable mortality and grief elicited a visceral reaction.

How many times have I walked into a hospital? It probably stretches into five figures. A few have been quite personal in nature: my children's birth, my mother's surgery, tests a doctor suggested I undergo, wondering if I might have something awful. Actually, all the visits are personal: I see people professionally, but I care for them, and often love them. Sometimes it's somebody I don't know, but very soon I know them quite intimately. A hospital brings out the best, and worst, in all of us. Pretensions are shed; politeness happens, but is irrelevant really. In hospitals, people arrive into this world, usually with glee and colored balloons, but not always. And in hospitals, people exit planet earth, or have their lives handed back to them. Others leave hospitals empty-handed, shriven, or else with the cured one in the car, grateful, not realizing in that moment of relief how swiftly the sheer fact of being alive will be taken for granted.

Losses happen lots of places, of course. I've never quite gotten over the loss of my extensive, hard-won baseball card collection (which my mother let go at a yard sale for $5), or the demise of my vinyl Beatles albums (which fell out of the car the day I moved to college, warping on the asphalt in the sweltering heat of August before I relocated them). The losses of family and friends, not to mention dreams and fantasies I'd harbored for my life—some things you just never get over. God must grieve, or assist in hidden ways. God knows where lost things are (like my Mickey Mantle rookie card, or the cross my friend Jim White gave me—and Mickey Mantle himself, or my friend Jim).

First Exposure to Death

What can I recall now about God in hospitals, and in times of devastating loss in and out of such institutions? Like most children, my first exposure to mortality was in the death of someone I didn't know—or rather, something. A bird thunked into the sliding glass door. My dad pronounced the creature dead, placed it in a shoebox, dug a hole, and muttered a few words to qualify it as a proper burial. I was sad, although I'd certainly stepped on a few ants without remorse or grief. Why do children love birds?

But then, like most children, my first real grief was when my dad picked us up in Oakboro and almost casually announced that Tiny, our mongrel dog, had died back home in Delaware. He might have been relieved to be rid of this dog who nipped and yapped too much. But I was numb, and then convulsed in grief. The questions that suggested themselves to me at age eight, I now realize, are the very questions grown people ask about the death of someone they love. *How could it be? Why wasn't I there?* Tiny had been struck by a car: but *What if I had been there?* Wouldn't he have been playing with me, and thus still be alive? Was he scared or in pain? Or was he just . . . gone? *Where was Tiny now?*—and I didn't mean *Was his body in a box in the backyard?* but rather *Is Tiny in some safe, happy place? Or just flat out, irrevocably vanished into oblivion?*

Of course, losses mount, and they grow in magnitude beyond a random bird or the pet who might be more beloved in the child's day to day life than human relatives who live in another state. Did God comfort me? I'd vote for yes, but how could one know such a thing? Perhaps God made me and all children with a kind of resilience, a bounceback buoyancy, that forgets the bird in a week and feels better about the dog when a new chihuahua shows up six months later.

Were these deaths God's will? Did God hurl the bird into the window? Or seize the steering wheel and crush poor Tiny? No child would think such a thing. You learn quite early that death is accidental; death has its randomness. Some of us forget this when we get older, or when we get more attached to those we love, and to God. But death just happens, it's not divinely mandated (thank God). And from the bird and the dog, and even the first human losses sustained, you really can move forward. You can get out of bed the next morning. There is more life, there is more laughter. And life is good, not merely in spite of the losses but, like some old painting whose beauty is a dance of darkness and light, actually discovered in the thick of the losses.

Once again, as must be the case for a large percentage of us, my first real grief over a real person was occasioned by the death of a grandparent: Papa Howell. I've narrated this sad story in chapter 2. As normal and frequent as death turns out to be, any one death seems utterly singular. If someone said "Get used to it," you might recoil in horror, or wave off such a thought, for the one death you grieve now is frankly as much as you can comprehend or even begin to cope with.

But then we begin to notice a stream of commonalities, and in surprising ways. Frederick Buechner has written more than once of his father's death—a suicide, and when Frederick was still called Freddy, just ten years old. A shout from downstairs. Panicked adults gathered around the garage door. A doctor was summoned. Days later a note was found, written on the last page of Gone With the Wind, addressed to Freddy's mother. "I adore and love you, and am no good . . . Give Freddy my watch. Give Jamie my pearl pin. I give you all my love."[1]

How fascinating: Buechner's loss breaks your heart, even if your father still has his watch and would never do such a thing. For you always suspect somewhere in the back of your soul that life really is fragile and even those who love you could leave you. That his father left, but yours stayed, bears considerable weight. You would never do such a thing yourself. But then again, who hasn't had a few moments when you wondered if it was worth your while to stick around—but then you did stick around?

1. Frederick Buechner, *The Sacred Journey* (San Francisco: Harper SanFrancisco, 1982), 41.

Nothing Can Make Up for the Absence

We always have friends with sunny dispositions who quickly and seemingly quite naturally "move on" after a tragic loss, who prefer to remember brighter days and grow impatient with much talk about suffering. They seem to know how to trump any ache with a smile, perhaps even to banish the darkness with a bright beacon of recovered happiness. I have never found myself to be very adept at this, and I am unsure why. I do know that sometimes the rush to "feel better" is so very American, so naïve, damaging psychologically—and the ruin of the kind of community and love the one who is hurting needs so desperately.

Consider something that transpired after one of the worst losses I have ever sustained. Molly McKay was a teenager in our church, one I knew well over several years, with an undeniable spark that was a catalyst for good things wherever she showed up. She swung by the church one August day on her way back to school for her third year at the University of North Carolina. All summer she had interned with our youth, and was exploring the possibilities of how to serve God with her life. We said goodbye the way people usually say goodbye—engaged, affectionate, but in retrospect too glib given what happened next. A westbound car on Interstate 40 bumped another westbound car, which lost control, lurched across the median, and hit Molly's car.

I got the call as I waited in a carpool line to pick up my daughters, who adored Molly. The next hours and days are a numb blur in my mind, but I remember hanging on to her father who had a hard time standing up, and to teenagers whose experience of loss had been limited to pets and grandparents.

That Sunday, a cloud dense with grief hung over our church family. We tried to worship, pray, and sing—and to gather our youth to cry and hang on to each other for dear life. But a mere week later, I got rattled when not just one but several folks came up to me after worship with deep, buoyant concern, and asked, "How are the McKays? Are they feeling better?" All I could stammer in reply was something like, "No, they aren't feeling better—and I'm not either."

Sympathizers always want to "say something," or "do something" to alleviate the pain. I was almost enraged when those folks could lamely fathom that a parent could conceivably "feel better" after a week—or a decade or two. Yet I did realize that in some ways I had tried quite a few ineffective balms on hurting people myself. What had I preached or gimpily offered in counseling? "Hurting? Jesus can help you feel better." People like these words. But is the cavernous space where the cold wind blows through my soul fixable? Wasn't God's glory manifest not when everyone felt better, but when on a pitch black afternoon Jesus wailed something at God about being forsaken?

And then, when I consider the lame, cruel truisms pious people offer to sufferers, I still shudder when I revisit the worst, the hardest, the most haunting funeral I ever conducted. ABC, CNN, all the local news stations: everyone showed up for the spectacle of the funeral of a small child, and the death was clearly the fault of the father. In a regrettable moment of inexplicable negligence, he left his precious son in the car, in the summer heat, the son he loved more than his own life. I have never seen so much sorrow up close.

We got through the service and then drove to the cemetery. After saying Amen to the closing prayer, I opened my eyes and saw a woman walking toward—me? No, toward the father standing next to me. She had a huge, broad smile on her face—surely the only person within a dozen square miles with any reason to smile on this darkest of days. Why was she smiling? So holy, so pious, so spiritual, she looked at this father who had just buried his son, and said, "You should rejoice. God took your child. God needed your child more than you did." He very calmly looked at her and said, "I don't believe that."

We don't believe that. God loves us. God would not kill our children, or kidnap them to live far away from us. God bears our suffering. God comes to redeem the worst losses we might ever endure. God is not the doer of evil, but the God who redeems evil.

But redemption doesn't mean grief doesn't or shouldn't linger. At age forty-nine, I reread Dietrich Bonhoeffer's *Letters and Papers from Prison*, and was thunderstruck by a letter I'd never noticed before. Bonhoeffer, who sat alone in a stone Nazi punishment cell on Christmas Eve of 1943, was reflecting upon family he had loved and lost, on his own fate and awful separation from his family. He wrote these jarring, eloquent words:

> Nothing can make up for the absence of someone we love, and it would be wrong to try to find a substitute; we must simply hold out and see it through. That sounds very hard at first, but at the same time it is a great consolation, for the gap, as long as it remains unfilled, preserves the bonds between us. It is nonsense to say God fills the gap; he doesn't fill it, but on the contrary, he keeps it empty and so helps us to keep alive our former communion with each other, even at the cost of pain . . . The dearer and richer our memories, the more difficult the separation. But

gratitude changes the pangs of memory into tranquil joy. The beauties of the past are borne, not as a thorn in the flesh, but as a precious gift in themselves.[2]

God keeps the gap open. Now I think I understand friends over the years who have been bludgeoned by the worst imaginable loss, the death of a child. Flailing numbly, they want to feel better, but in their heart of hearts they have no wish to feel better—for the pain is the place where a son, a daughter now lives on. To move on, to forget, would be to stash that most precious of gifts away in a closet someplace.

The wisest book I have read on grief is *A Lament for a Son*, written by the Yale philosopher Nicholas Wolterstorff, in the aftermath of the mountain-climbing death of his twenty-five-year old son, Eric. Several years after this horrible loss, Wolterstorff noticed that the wound "is no longer raw. But it has not disappeared. That is as it should be. If he was worth loving, he is worth grieving over. Grief is existential testimony to the worth of the one loved . . . Every lament is a love-song."[3]

Who Can See the Top of His Head?

I could sing a concert of such love-songs for you, lamenting quite a few losses I've sustained, and your list may put mine in the shade. During seminary, I visited daily with a classmate, Thaniel, slowly losing the battle she was waging just to breathe before cystic fibrosis took her from us. On the day the doctor ran up his white flag of surrender, declaring "There's nothing more we can do," I am embarrassed now to admit that I had a hard time making eye contact with my friend—but she reached out her hand to me, and said "James, it's okay. Jesus loves me, and I love Jesus, and it is enough."

We might hear this and feel soothed, or safer somehow—that someone treading a road we hope to avoid forever but fear we might find ourselves on actually still believed, and coped, and flourished as vitally as possible. But there were darker days to come, moments of anger, and doubt. Harder still was all this for Thaniel's mother. During one particularly bleak night at the Duke Medical Center, I was sitting with her and her mother, agonizing with her as she fought for the most shallow of breaths. Her pain was relentless. When I stood up to leave, her mother was standing over by

2. Dietrich Bonhoeffer, *Letters and Papers from Prison*, ed. Eberhard Bethge (New York: Macmillan, 1971), 176.

3. Nicholas Wolterstorff, *Lament for a Son* (Grand Rapids: Eerdmans, 1987), 5.

the window, looking out at—well, at nothing at all. The panes exposed the blackness of the night, nothing more. Pitifully I asked, "Would you like for me to say a prayer?" Her barely audible reply made me shudder. "Pray if you wish. Nobody's listening."

At that moment I was engulfed by the gloom. Now, in retrospect, I think I can see God in that room, or out the window, and the God I see is the one revealed on the cross when Jesus was battling hard for each breath, with his mother watching (or perhaps averting her gaze, so horrid must have been her ache); when he gathered himself enough to speak, he groaned out loud some words his mother had actually taught him when he was a little boy—from the Psalms: "My God, my God, why have you forsaken me?" The Gospel writers remembered God, or the grim, appalling absence of God, and I remember Thaniel, and her mother, and that dark night.

More stories come to mind of friends, family, even people I've just read about in the newspaper. What did John Donne say? "Every man's death diminishes me"? What is the cumulative effect of one after another? How did my friend Pat feel—Pat, who lived deep into her nineties, long enough to lose just about everybody, her husband, all three children, and most of her friends?

We're not left with much, except Thomas Merton's thought, which is more than a thought but honestly the truest, most brutal yet hopeful solace: reflecting on the inevitable losses we suffer, he wrote (in a letter to Dorothy Day) that persevering in our relationship with God isn't

> a matter of getting a bulldog grip on faith and not letting the devil pry us loose from it. No, it is a matter of letting go rather than keeping hold. I am coming to think God . . . loves and helps best those who are so beat and have so much nothing when they come to die that it is almost as if they had persevered in nothing but had gradually lost everything, piece by piece, until there was nothing left but God . . . It is a question of his hanging on to us, by the hair of the head, that is from on top and beyond, where we cannot see or reach. What man can see the top of his own head?[4]

How many times, indeed, have I bowed my head, not in noble piety, and certainly not as a grinning optimist, but in the desperation that alone understands grace and mercy? It is at the heart of God's mercy that we do not

4. Paul Elie, *The Life You Save May Be Your Own* (New York: Farrar, Straus and Giroux, 2003), 301.

have to avert our gaze from suffering. In fact, we look, and in the place of agony we discover Christ—who after all, knew our griefs, died our death, wept, and cried out in his moment of glory.

As a pastor, I get to spend a much higher than average amount of time with people who are dying. Notice I said "get to." Every now and then some parishioner, expressing concern, will say "I don't know how you do your job; I can imagine you could burn out after a few years of watching people suffer up close." But this well-intended thought could not be more wrong. I may burn out one day, but it will be because of the small-minded who feel some obligation to nit-pick and grouse about trivialities, those combative sorts who keep everyone bent out of shape over an insignificant budget item, or what color the carpet should be in the ladies' parlor.

To be with any person in the hour of death, to pull up a chair and hold the hand of someone who is digesting frightening news from the oncologist, to sit late at night with a family as they concede there is little time left, to listen to tender words, to offer a tissue to help wipe away tears blackened by makeup, to hug someone who is trembling, and to overhear defiant words of hope: this is the part of the life of a minister I would not live without. Not because I am a great giver or helper: generally I feel utterly useless. I always wish I could utter some sentence or wave a wand of healing; but all I know how to do is quite simply to show up and wait it out, sitting in as a paltry but determined representative of the church family and perhaps even of God Almighty.

This is the privilege: as a pastor, I get to see the nobility of humanity, to be there when words that matter are spoken. Grown children kiss their father, perhaps for the first time since turning eight or nine. Friends dispense of more polite verbiage and say "I love you." Grandchildren sit on the edge of the bed and perhaps get to ride up and down, the one dying knows we can't go to the amusement park again, but at least we can ride this gurney a time or two. God's grace is palpable, unforgettable, not nearly as effective as any of us might wish, hard to see, but mystifyingly, almost solidly there. Lovers and the beloved understand what Merton meant by being beat and having lost everything and being hung onto by the top of the head.

The Night I Decided to Quit

And yet it is easier to write these words about it being such a "privilege" than to share the pain when the privilege is debilitating, and the sense of uselessness crushing. Intellectually I realize I am often as helpless as those I've come to help, and that my vocation is simply to show up. But a lifetime of showing up without making much of a difference is taxing, verging onto a kind of depression, and I've wondered more often than I'll ever admit even to myself, *Why bother?*

One chilly night I decided to quit. Quit the ministry, quit hospitals, quit trying to matter. It began on a bright morning. My day off. The phone rang—and I have a congenital anxiety that a phone ringing just may have some horrible announcement on the other end if I pick up. Usually it's a salesperson—but you never know. That morning, the ringing turned out to be what John Irving called a "burglar alarm of the heart." It was the chaplain at a nearby hospital. Usually we would exchange pleasantries, but all she said was, "Come to the hospital—now." I trusted the urgency in her voice and arrived in about ten minutes. I found her with a young couple from our church whom I knew and loved. I sensed lingering echoes of shrieks and sobs in the room, which was now eerily silent. After only the briefest passing eye contact, the wife and then the husband fell onto my shoulders. I could hardly bear their weight as they gasped for words. Caroline, whom I had baptized only a couple of weeks earlier, had just been diagnosed with a malignant tumor intertwined with her spinal cord at the base of the brain. I couldn't parse the news.

Then a man in a white coat said, "We must go to Duke Medical Center—now." "Now" had been uttered twice. "Of course I will come too," I assured them. The drive took forever, or maybe it was a few seconds. Time forgot how to pass properly. Engulfed by Duke's massive medical center, we were shuffled from one waiting room to another. No one spoke, and I felt particularly conspicuous for not speaking. *Say something!* I kept telling myself. Read a Bible verse, offer a prayer—something. But all I could do was cry, and then I would go numb, alternating helplessly between the two.

Another minister who knew the family materialized. His demeanor startled me: smiling, confident, speaking many words, assuring the parents with an utterly confident grin that "God will save your child if you just pray." I'm ordained, he's ordained—but I felt no kinship with him. I oscillated between wanting to strangle him and wanting to be more like him. Why have I never been able to be pious? When did I become the grim pastor who expects the worst? Sure, his style of pastoring seemed trite, absurd—but he was doing something. What good was I doing?

About that time, the pediatric oncologist came in—calm, intelligent, well-trained, impressive. I remember him as being very tall. He had a plan. As he unfolded his strategy, I remembered those smart grown-ups who had advised me to go to medical school. And I wished I had, because as a minister I had nothing—literally—to offer to these people I loved so much. Had I gone to medical school, I could do something. I kept listening to him, hanging on every word, envy rising, regret surging. Not only should I have gone to medical school; I should not have gone into the ministry. I felt so impotent. I realized that I spent most of my days praying for people having gall bladders removed laparoscopically, or knees replaced metallically, and how ridiculously invaluable my parishioners regarded me because of it. But here was a family in dire need, and I had nothing, absolutely nothing, to give. Reduced to tears, sitting in the corner, I knew some clever chap would console me by saying, "It's the ministry of presence: you're the embodiment of God's church!" But Caroline's parents desperately craved one thing only: the life of their daughter.

So I decided to resign and do something else—anything else—for the rest of my working life. The details were fuzzy, but I knew I couldn't live out the charade of praying for head colds and pacemaker installations when I was undeniably impotent in the face of real peril. More tests were run. Surgery would be required early in the morning. The initial rush of family and friends began to drift away to other waiting areas. Some returned home. Caroline, repeatedly poked and prodded, had been crying incessantly all afternoon and evening. Why was I still there? Then her parents asked me for a favor. "We are exhausted. Caroline won't stop crying. Could you hold her for a little while so we can step out and take a little break?" And so I took this child in my arms and rocked her. She cried, and I cried, and then, having expended all her energy, she drifted off to sleep. I kept rocking her until her parents came back, a little bit rested, relieved to see her more peaceful. We placed her gently in the crib, and then I left them, took the elevator downstairs, and stepped through the door into the night.

As I felt the chill against my face, I changed my mind, and recovered a bit of myself. I would not quit the ministry. It was as if my whole life had been a preparation for this dark evening. All the wrestling with what career to pursue, counsel from professors, the books, papers, degrees, hurdles of ordination: I had been in training for this day, so that on this day I could drive to Durham and give two parents a little bit of rest—and to rock a very sick child to sleep, just to hold this little one who seemed to have as little hope as I did.

Struck from Behind

It was around midnight that I had to answer a question: Why did I go into the ministry? To do something grand and impressive? Or because I thought I might love somebody, some family, some child, in God's name? Holding Caroline, I wondered: isn't this what Mary did with Jesus when he was sick during the night? Didn't she embrace him when he was taken down from the cross? Isn't this what God Almighty had been doing with me all these years? And on one night, I was able to help. I held a child. I fulfilled my vocation, the small impotence of it all turning out to be the beauty.

The hallways of a medical center, and all the trillion places where things and loves are lost, raise a river of questions, the primal one being *How much is enough? How long is long enough? How much suffering can we take? How many years would have been sufficient to have loved, and lived?* Perhaps it's never enough, even if we manage to befriend death and die gracefully, or let her go with a subdued joy and release into the hands of God. How strange is it, that in the darkest throes of grief, people report later how palpable was their sense of God's presence?

Paul wrote that "Love never ends" (1 Corinthians 13)—but what really happens to the love? It is tested—sternly. In Rian Malan's marvelous book about Apartheid in South Africa, *My Traitor's Heart*, Creina Alcock has suffered much; late in life, she says,

> Love is worth nothing until it has been tested by its own defeat. Love, even if it ends in defeat, gives you a kind of honor; without love, you have no honor at all. Love enables you to transcend defeat. Love is the only thing that leaves light inside you, instead of the total, obliterating darkness.[5]

I fear the obliteration of darkness. And I could pile up stories of pain and loss where I've been observer, embracer, midwife of a little survival, and even shreds of hope. What intrigues me, for all my facility at coping with misery and death, are the surprises when life unbelievably, inexplicably, and rather absurdly, yet therefore all the more happily emerges out of the pit of darkness. So let me tell you about a few "coincidences," although you might prefer to call them "miracles." I can never be sure.

---

5. Rian Malan, *My Traitor's Heart: A South African Exile Returns to Face His Country, His Tribe, and His Conscience* (New York: Vintage, 1990), 409.

Chapter 7

Miracles

The Vision, and Life Support

STUFF HAPPENS. BELIEVERS PUT far too much stock in mere coincidence, but I do not. I understand: we crave some proof of the divine, we really could use some direction from God, some order or purpose in the chaos of it all. But my analysis suggests that people notice a coincidence, and find therein the sign they were looking for. I would vastly prefer my parishioners make decisions and believe what they believe about God because of the coincidence of the prayers of the liturgy with the scripture readings and our inherited treasury of belief and the exemplary lives of the saints, rather than an imposed spin on some haphazard happening.

So when it comes to random coincidence in daily life, I side with the atheist evolutionist Richard Dawkins, who said that if our head spins over some chance occurrence, "what we need is less gasping and more thinking."[1] Do the math: coincidences just happen, and all the time. Explaining chance isn't hard if you use your brain. The chance may feel knee-buckling when a drunk driver hits, out of thousands of cars on the road, the one car driven by the one I loved and could not imagine living without. But believing God arranged this coincidence crushes all consolation. So we look to the Bible and the sacraments—the means of grace, a grace well-conceived and trustworthy. Let's apply critical thinking to stave off superstition and find grace where we are supposed to find it.

1. Richard Dawkins, *Unweaving the Rainbow: Science, Delusion and the Appetite for Wonder* (Boston: Houghton Mifflin, 1998), 147.

But then something happens. Or I should say, something happened, and either I pretend it didn't really happen, or I tell it and risk dubious raised eyebrows among rationalists like myself, or wide grins from the spiritually intuitive. Either way, I feel like the fool in a Flannery O'Connor story.

The Baptismal Vision

In my forties, I had a friend named Clay. Single, a gastroenterologist, a ferocious competitor at spades, a loner content to sit on the back pew, occasionally volunteering for medical mission work. He called one day: "Can you come over? I have something to show you." In his den, on the floor, was a basinet. With a baby inside.

Clay had gone to Oklahoma and adopted a little girl. I had never imagined him as a dad, but in the ensuing months of watching him, I felt like I had discovered a new wing in a museum, harboring its most stunning treasures. A marvelous dad he was, and his daughter Lauren returned the favor. Like Silas Marner when he found a girl with curls instead of his gold, Clay could well have been described by George Eliot's words: the child "stirred quiverings of tenderness, impressions of some power presiding over his life . . . [She] called him away from his weaving, and made him think all its pauses a holiday, reawakening his senses with her fresh life, warming him into joy because she had joy."[2]

Never have I seen a dad more delighted than Clay when he brought Lauren to the font for her baptism. After the service, a woman who had never met Clay called to tell me, "I had a vision during that baptism." Patiently I listened to yet one more of the kinds of syrupy stories I've heard so many times. "The roof of the building lifted off, and light streamed down on the child from heaven, and a host of angels from heaven gathered around the font." I thanked her, I hope not as dismissively as I might have felt, and then promptly forgot about it.

For five years, that is. One night Clay, who had since moved to Texas, called. He had just been diagnosed with brain cancer. The doctors predicted he would only live a few months. I shuddered not once but twice: the prospect of losing my friend, and then the thought of Lauren, about to start kindergarten, losing her only parent. After a restless night, I went to work the next day. Opening my mail, I found a notecard—from the woman who'd had the vision at the baptism five years earlier. She had thought

2. George Eliot, *Silas Marner* (New York: Bantam, 1981), 112, 128.

about it again, and had commissioned an artist to paint what she had seen. Then she had the painting made into notecards, and she thought I'd want to see one.

Now I have tried to do the math and to calculate the odds of this woman happening to have her lone baptismal vision during this particular baptism, the odds of this card arriving in my mail not two years later, and not eight years later, but five years later, and not within a month or so of my hearing Clay's news, but the morning after (meaning she actually put it in the mail the same day he learned of his diagnosis)—and although I know Richard Dawkins would mount some explanation, I figured the odds against this being random are literally astronomical. But what was the meaning of this? Hesitantly I told a friend, whose face lit up as he said, "He's going to be healed!" How I wish that had been the case. Clay died on a cold winter day. Lauren had not reached her seventh birthday yet.

I flew to Texas to preach his funeral, with the notecard with the light and the angels tucked in my bag, unsure whether to show it or even mention it. I had gotten more cards from the woman with the vision, and had even shown one to Clay before he died. Like me, he was a skeptic about such matters. Should I say something about the notecard during his funeral? And if so, what?

In the pulpit, looking over Clay's casket, noting this was the first time he'd been at the front of the church instead of the back pew, I spoke (of course) of the gospel, making a few points out of Clay's life and loves. I finished and started to sit down, and then it occurred to me that to withhold the evidence I held, no matter how confused I might be about its meaning, would be to slam a window shut when we really could use some light. So

Struck from Behind

I told them about the card, the vision, and precisely when it came in the mail. A jaw or two dropped, a few people nodded; one man rolled his eyes.

I admitted, "I do not know what this means, but it has to mean something. Perhaps when Lauren was baptized, the dark shadow in Clay's head that would eventually lengthen and be his undoing was perceived by the God we invoked in worship. And perhaps that same God, who is never happy to leave such a shadow to be nothing but darkness, flashed a small light in another head, in the mind of someone Clay did not even know, so that now, in this dark moment, we might see a small flicker of a candle, some intimation of grace, bridging space and time so we might detect that goodness of a God whose light does shine in the darkness."

Doesn't our theology require us to believe that in baptism, this child—no, these children, Clay in his baptism decades before, and Lauren just six years prior to his death, are sealed with the Spirit, are claimed by a God whose power manifests itself in the liturgy and scripture, but also in the minds and hearts of all kinds of folk and in the most surprising of places? Isn't grace sneaky like that, tiptoeing up behind us in the dark, making no sense whatsoever? What an interesting miracle: not the cure we were praying for, but no less miraculous—a stranger's vision, and a card in hand.

As I grow older, I am trying to develop this underdeveloped, intuitive side of my own befuddled self. Since Clay's death, I find myself listening more attentively to people who tell me of their faith experiences, knowing some are sheer quirkiness, but alert to signs of grace nonetheless. Now I look for God in curious circumstances. I've been prepared for the roof to come off the building at any moment. I began looking for miracles—and I would need one.

Life Support

"I'm going to see Shane." Common enough in those days for my daughter to say as she turned at the bottom of the stairs to head for her car. This time it felt a tad strange, not the words, but the tone of it, almost as if her quiver betrayed a worry. Turns out she'd phoned him quite a few times, with no response. Explanations presented themselves: his phone is dead, he's sound asleep and it's on silent, he's at work where there's a lousy signal, he lost his phone again. But such ready-made reasons have a timer on them, and when the alarm finally sounds, you know you need to know, and now—so she was headed to his place to find, hopefully, Shane asleep, or doing whatever it is people do when they don't pick up the phone.

Impatient, although more patient than I'd ever been in such circumstances, while still driving she phoned his dad, who went to his son's place—and discovered the horrifying reason: he wasn't picking up because he could not, because he was unconscious, because he was barely alive, totally nonresponsive. The ambulance came, Grace was rerouted to the hospital, and she texted me with a dreamily optimistic or dreadfully denying text: "Shane's in the hospital; it might be serious."

I drove as rapidly as possible, found the ER, hoping it was all mere panic, nothing unfixable wrong with this young man I'd grown to love. But the eyes of the chaplain who greeted us betrayed the immensity of the peril. I'd been to enough critical situations in dozens of hospitals to know things were dire, that life hung in the balance, and we were reduced to the helpless posture of those who wait, heads spinning, unwittingly steeled by a numbness that refused to think what was obvious.

News, hints, preliminary diagnoses, and guesses trickled in from gravely concerned physicians and nurses. Medical terminology, some terms we might have overheard from some TV show, others utterly foreign, washed over us: strokes, oxygen deprivation, stem functions. The important questions, in fact the lone important question, could not even be raised—but I pulled the attending physician aside and asked what parents dared not ask: "Will he make it?" Grimly the doctor sighed and said, "It's 50/50—at best." A weirdly, almost obnoxiously chipper man with a badge—what was his job? maybe another chaplain?—suggested we might confidently put this in God's hands.

I sensed the looks of family peering my way. *He's a pastor, right? He knows how to pray, how to get God to help.* But as always in such situations, my healing powers were not just suspect but shabbily lame. All I could do was fight back tears. I mumbled some words when everyone's eyes were closed, and my quivering voice exposed my deep chagrin and instilled no confidence whatsoever.

The course of events that evening, as I try to recall them, is kooky, cloudy, crazed, befuddling. I was trying to be strong, determined to be a rock for my daughter, and her boyfriend's parents. But then I found myself walking back toward the ward, trying my clergy access card—and was alone in the hallway outside intensive care. To my surprise—although why was I surprised?—I collapsed to my knees and sobbed, out loud, heaves of tears, gulping for air, a swoon, the horror of it all sinking in. We were about to lose this lovely, polite, fun, precious young man who'd been the first to love my daughter who'd had more than enough to deal with in her short life already. He had given her life and hope when I hadn't known how to. He was the guy who believed in her when nobody else did, who felt immensely lucky just to be at her side.

How to Pray?

I prayed, and desperately—and I had to preface my pleas by reminding God I hadn't asked for much in my life. This is not because I've been noble, but because I'm an intellectual, or rather, a realist about prayer. My skepticism isn't entirely a result of my stellar education or a scientific bent in my mentality. My profession has been to sit with people in the gloomiest circumstances. I've prayed over hundreds, maybe thousands of people—and I know better than anyone else that miracles just don't happen much—if ever. The doctors are always right, and if there's a cure, it's not a heavenly intervention but the good results of surgeries, medications, and physician brilliance—and so we thank God for good medical care.

My calling, my gift to sufferers, has always been my realism, my ability to recognize that pancreatic cancer just doesn't get better, that Alzheimers patients never recover their faculties, that brains deprived of oxygen are lost to us forever, and God is still there, God never lets us go, God redeems—and we have an eternity to look forward to after the miseries of what doctors cannot cure. People want to reject God because God didn't shelter them or those they love from harm; but I know how to stir faith in them anyhow—and part of that is by not asking so daringly and uncompromisingly for a cure.

So I hadn't asked God for much, and I wished in all candor I'd always been a very different kind of minister, the kind that can smile and believe in the slim potential for a divine cure in the face of the worst diagnosis. How could I, of all people, pray in such a place and in this hour?

To make matters worse—or that is, make my praying even more impossible, and adding an edge of rage to whatever I might pray—I recalled that months earlier I actually *had* prayed for something quite specific, repeatedly, never expecting fulfillment: I had prayed that God would somehow bring my daughter a good boyfriend. She'd been through so much, she never was in situations where she might meet guys at all, much less good guys. Never expecting a happy result, for some reason I'd prayed for a positive, loving boyfriend—and Shane had rather miraculously (or so even I had come to believe) appeared in my driveway, in our den, in our lives, a wonder, totally unexpected, as against the odds as a cure of pancreatic cancer or brain trauma.

So, as I tried in agony to speak with God about this out in the hallway, I spouted crazed accusations and pleas to the God I thought might be listening, but seemed to be quite typically unhelpful just now. *How could you answer that former prayer, bringing Shane into our lives, only to lose him now?* Some heavenly cruelty, a dastardly evil in the very answer to prayer, seemed to cloud the bare attempt to pray for help now: wouldn't it have been better if he'd never come, if that prayer had simply been left to flutter about like so many other pipe dream prayers? *Why, if you are a God with a glimmer of love and tenderness, let such a wonderful person into our lives only to let him slip away?* Yes, I knew rationally there were reasons why such things transpire. But the jarring clash of it all, the absurdity of bothering to pray now, reduced me to the edge of nothingness.

Like all who pray in such darkened hallways, I begged, I bargained, I urged God to make just this one exception, to help perhaps just a little. I went into Shane's room, and grasped his head, where so much seemed to have been lost, and tried to let a holy power I knew nothing about flow through me into him. Shane's dad watched me hopefully. I admitted, "I don't really know how to do this, but I've got to try."

Days went by, and Shane was almost totally inert, motionless, alive only due to the beeping of machines we'd learned more about than we'd cared to know. A doctor read an MRI and spoke of removing life support. Strokes—eight of them—were visible on the screens for us to see. He might live, but he would never be himself. He would never walk out of the hospital or return to anything resembling his former life.

Funny thing about hospitals, in such dire straits. Family and friends set up shop, almost like decorating, making it as homey as possible; usually I visit professionally, but now this waiting room was my home too. Somebody's always there, covering a shift, waves drifting in and then back out. You make small talk, you do busy little nothings, you even tell silly jokes—all to hold the reality at bay.

For the reality is too heavy, or downright crushing. Gravity seems to work harder than normal. You feel the floor won't hold you up much longer, as if you might plunge clean through and plummet through the basement and foundations into some dark abyss. The moorings of up and down spiral about your head, your knees turn to ice, and mere tears would be a welcome relief from the intensity of the geyser of grief that can't be calmed.

My realism kicked in, and I began to accept things, practiced as I've become over decades at bracing myself and others for the inevitable. I scanned my calendar to assess funeral availability. I wondered about legal questions in the wake of death. I mostly tried to keep my mind busy so as not to think about Grace, and the immensity, the irreversibility of such a blindingly horrible loss.

The Unbelievable

And then. Thank God I can begin this paragraph with those two words and their sunny hopefulness: "And then." Days passed. I was impressed by Shane's dad, never giving up hope, talking to him constantly, giving him directions like "Squeeze my hand, Shane. Wake up, Shane." Over and over, and over. After four days, somebody was holding Shane's hand, not asking him to do anything in particular, and there was a small squeeze. "You're making it up, it's just wishful thinking." But then we began to stare very carefully, without blinking, at his inert body, and most assuredly there was a little twitch here, a little movement there.

And then—his eye opened a little. I snapped a photo with my phone. The nurse assured us this just happens, it doesn't mean anything. But on the third day of his eye being opened, we felt quite sure he was seeing us, tracking movement. Did we dare let our hopes rise up? And then he rose up: not in response to being asked, he sat bolt upright in the bed one day, eliciting the kinds of shrieks kids yelp when frightened on Halloween. A squeeze of the hand, or an eye tracking you could always be questioned. But rising up in the bed, and before witnesses?

Others began to take photos, and (I'm a little embarrassed to say) posted them on Facebook, to chart his progress, and to let the world know that this one who was lost was somehow found, that the dead really did seem to be rising again. The championship photo was one Grace took the day Shane shocked everybody by—standing. With assistance, of course, but standing. The next day, a step, then another step. His mind was enveloped in some thick cloud, but every day a little bit of the fog lifted. He began to try to speak, and then to make sounds, and finally to fashion a word, then words, then sentences. He made no sense, but we did not care. He was back with us, sentient, if only a little. He seemed, even if shrouded a bit, his old self, excessively polite, naturally grateful, picking on others in his good natured way.

Startled by this unexpected, unexplainable climb out of the grave back into life, my cynical side kept wondering, *When will the progress cease?* He had endured eight strokes; the doctor said he'd never walk. For weeks he was with us, but barely; he spoke but made no sense; he walked to the bathroom but it took an hour to get there. But gradually he became quicker, more nimble; his sentences grew in coherence. He walked down the hall, then outside, and even hit a few golf balls. Then a few weeks later played a full round of golf. The highway department let him have his driver's license back, and only those who knew him best could detect even the slightest alteration from his pre-trauma manner of being.

As I had failed to show up to preach the first Sunday morning of this ordeal, when it appeared he would live only another hour or two, his situation was pretty public. Dozens, or more likely hundreds of people were praying for him—the way we often pray, just doing it to show love, or naively hoping against hope, or sunnily expecting good news when there really won't be any good news at all. So when Shane lived, and then exited the hospital, and showed up at church, people were stunned, delighted, and cheerfully proclaimed, "It's a miracle!"

Everyone said so—except me. How could I say it was a miracle, when I live with and pastor so many people who've prayed intently for the lengthening of life, only to have the one they loved die far earlier than the doctors had predicted? And yet, how could I say it was not a miracle? I knew the odds, had witnessed the physician's grim demeanor—and I knew my own raging, panicked, pleading prayers. How do any of us assess such things?

What I do know with absolute certainty is that I saw my daughter at her noblest—almost as if she had been created by God for such a time as this. When she was a little girl, on the few occasions that I was sick (or the semi-humorous time I tore my hamstring trying to cling to my youth by playing full-court basketball), Grace was the one who sat by my bedside, brought me toast, daubed my forehead with a cool cloth. Shane was critically ill, and in the early hours she was as tearful and numb as the rest of us.

But from the very first slight sign of hope, she became the true believer. She believed he would recover—and fully. Even when we thought, *Well, he'll live but never get out and about,* she kept insisting he'd get back near 100 percent. She was the one in the hospital who sat with him, helped him think, eat, relearn how to talk. She was unfathomably patient when he made those twenty-foot treks to the bathroom that lasted an hour. Here was my Grace, who'd battled much and suffered a tediously quirky round of bad health and luck for quite a few years, rising to the hardest of occasions, heroic, tender—all grace, I'm tempted to say, and no one could fault me for speaking of it in such a grand way.

Grateful for this, I think of Shane's recovery. Was it a miracle? When I get to heaven, my first question may well be, "Lord, did you do that?" I cannot fathom the answer will be No. But then I'll have quite a few harder questions to ask.

Bearing Fruit

We will speak in chapter 10 about "gifts," when it will become clear that the most stunning, memorable, grace-full gifts are given and received in the nexus of loss. I once heard Allen Verhey give a lecture about a historic, tragic turn in the way we human beings die. Once upon a time, people died at home. So the one nearing death would hold court, with some drama and tenderness. Family and neighbors would visit, and the nearly deceased could say *Take care of the chickens for me,* or *I forgive you for letting my cows get away* (or for getting drunk and wrecking my truck). Now we die in an alien place, sterile, with limited visiting hours, tubes blocking the part of us that might forgive, or give last-minute instructions.

Henri Nouwen, in his lovely book *Our Greatest Gift,* asks how we might be fruitful in our latter days. Not productive, but fruitful. When we no longer can work or earn, we can still be fruitful, by speaking words that will be recalled, by dying in a way that is a gift to the living. I was blessed to be befriended by Dr. Claude Broach late in his life. After a storied career as a "good Baptist" minister and champion of things ecumenical, he retired to my neighborhood, and we enjoyed regular lunches and lovely conversation. When he was in his final days, I paid him a visit and asked how it was for him: having ushered hundreds of his church members through their last moments, what was he thinking and feeling in his final days? His answer was twofold: "Well, I am curious." After the word "curious" lingered in the room for a minute, he added: "Mostly I am focused on the person of Jesus. All the theology I've read, all the talk about denominations and church structures—that's all a blur now. It's the person, Jesus."

As I move through time, I find I too am curious. Okay, perhaps anxious, but there is a holy core of curiosity tucked away inside the more debilitating mood of anxiety. I am curious about my own end, which may already have happened by the time you are reading these words. As I'm typing, I am fifty-six and in good health. Do I have thirty years left? Or thirty days? Will my demise come quickly? Or will it be long and drawn out? Which to hope for? Not too quickly, but not too long and drawn out, and certainly not with the ravages of chronic illness, as I'm a sissy about pain and nausea, and really prefer not to be a bother to family and friends. But these are not choices granted to us.

I would hope and pray that my dying might be fruitful, or at least that my living will prove to have been fruitful. I wonder if I shall be curious or just plain scared? When I was in seminary, I wrote a paper on the *Testament of Abraham*, one of those little obscure writings from biblical times that didn't make it into the Bible, or even the Apocrypha—but what a lovely tale. The writer imagines Abraham in old age, and he hears a knock at the door. A stranger. Abraham always knew what to do when a stranger called. Hospitality was always Abraham's middle name—and so he welcomed him in. Yet this stranger turned out to be the angel of death; Abraham embraced into his own home the one who came to take his life.

When death visits, will I welcome him? Or slam the door, flip the dead bolt (ha!), and jam a chair to keep the guy out? Will I rage (with Dylan Thomas) against the dying of the light, not going gently? Or will I be more placid, perhaps like Claude Broach or the holy host of martyrs or even Jesus himself, and go gently, perhaps reciting the Psalm Jesus recalled from the cross—"Father, into your hands I commit my spirit"?

Goin' Home to Live Wid' God

In 2005, Bishop McCleskey asked me to preach our annual memorial service for clergy who had died in the past year. I tried to say something about death being beautiful, because the death of Jesus, our brother and our Lord, is beautiful. I think that is right, hope it is right. Then I eased back from mystical theology and told an old joke that perhaps only clergy appreciate. Two clergy meet in the afterlife. One says, "Hey, compared to parish ministry, heaven is great!" And the other minister says, "Uh, this isn't heaven."

Then I spoke of the inevitable disappointments of ministry, one being that we are swiftly forgotten. I shared that I had run into a man who was a member of a church I'd served. "Cool," I said; "I used to be the minister there." He looked puzzled and asked, "What's your name?" "James

Struck from Behind

Howell." He squinted a little and said, "I don't know . . ." I smiled pleasantly and restrained myself from saying "I poured twelve years of my life, heart, soul and blood into that church, and I've only been gone four years!"

That is how it unfolds: as a clergyperson you get invited back for a homecoming, you notice your photograph in the gallery of rogues in the hallway. People are mildly happy to see you—but then they dive into the pork and beans and fried chicken, chattering about whatever is more current in their life than you, the old fossil. Oblivion. A few more years, and no one will remember. Just a picture on the wall among many.

I had intended to leave some profound mark on the church, never to be forgotten. I'd longed to be a modern-day John Chrysostom, a fiery prophetic force that would change the world. But I drifted. We all drift into certain oblivion—and the drift is toward being *lost in wonder, love and praise*. I recalled the embarrassment of being one of only two boys in my high school chorus—but then the delight in going to some regional honors chorus where there were dozens, maybe hundreds of boys. What did we sing? That old spiritual, "Soon ah will be done ah—wid de troubles ob' de worl,'" and all of us boys rang out together singing loudly, "Goin' home to live wid God." Sooner than we think, we're going home. Here's how I ended the sermon, and I hope this is how I shall end my days too:

> As clergy down here, you have to be a single voice, and it gets lonely lots of days. Knowing our one voice will be forgotten, we leave it behind: take care of my chickens; take care of my church. And then we walk through the door—the way an individual grape, or a single grain of wheat drifts into the oblivion of a cask of wine and a loaf of bread, and on the table becomes the body and blood of our Lord. Or the way a small drop of water, a tear, or the mist, joins an innumerable host of other droplets of water, and I become part of a cloud, just a drop in a cloud of witnesses, and it is at the very end of the day, as the sun returns to its resting place, that the drops, the cloud, refracts the light of the sun and multiplies itself into stunning hues, a dazzling dance of stunning color, the glory of God almighty, the beauty we only know as darkness descends.

Chapter 8

The Baptists Tried to Kill Me
Jesus said, Follow Me

MOST OF THIS BOOK is devoted to remembering God in all the less than obvious ways, and in places and events that are not explicitly religious. But there is a crucial story line, the twisting, curious, surprising, unflattering and wonderful saga of how I came to be a Christian, not something pasted on the outside of an otherwise secular life, but the one story line that makes sense of the rest. My relationship with God has been constant—on God's side, that is. My awareness of God, or even my interest in bothering with God, would be choppy, even embarrassing, with fits and starts, and long periods of nothing really. So I am all the more grateful that in adult life I've been dogged about my life of faith, although most days I still feel like I did trying to learn to ride a bicycle: falling down a lot, but getting back on the thing, determined one day to get some balance and movement, enjoying the breeze despite scraped knees, and hopefully going somewhere.

I was not baptized as an infant. I was never an acolyte or a crucifer. I never once went to any youth group, or Christian camp. I had never heard of Confirmation. I owned a Bible, a black leather King James Version that Santa left under the tree when I was five—a bit of an optimistic gift to give to a little boy too young to read any English at all, much less the King's English. I had been to church—and as best I can recall, the churches in question were usually Southern Baptist. My mother was reared Methodist, my dad Baptist—and I suspect she chose to try the Baptists hoping he would get involved, or maybe even reformed. I am quite sure that she was always the kind of Methodist who really is a Baptist at heart.

Struck from Behind

The Baptists Tried to Kill Me

I never know how what to say about the Baptists. Ecumenism has always mattered immensely to me. Friendships across denominational boundaries must be pleasing to God, a small intimation of how things will be in heaven. But while I've befriended a few Baptists, I have found many to be too syrupy, self-assured and well-coiffed for my tastes. Quite a few strike me as narrow, judgmental, and a bit intimidating. In fact, the Baptists tried to kill me—twice!—before saving my life—twice!—or actually thrice.

In 1963, our family moved to Dover, Delaware for my father's last stint in the Air Force. Delaware struck me, a Georgia native who'd never seen snow and thought all trees were draped with moss, as the far north. Near our home, though, was a *Southern* Baptist Church; they seemed to be everywhere. The details are sketchy in my mind, but somehow I was at a revival meeting, and got the daylights scared out of me by some guest evangelist of the hellfire and brimstone variety. So, at the tender, theologically unreflective age of eight, I found myself not walking but sprinting to the front during the first stanza of the altar call, "Just As I Am." The preacher was gleeful that one so young had come to faith in Christ.

But I would never, ever have gone up, no matter how scary the devil and eternal flames might have been, had I known what was next. I was to be baptized. I didn't know what that was, but when you're eight you do as you're told. They led me through a door at the front, up a short flight of steps—and behold, back down a few more steps there was a small tank, a pool a bit larger than my bathtub at home. A curtain opened, and people saw me wading into this pool with the pastor whom they called Brother Adams. He said a few things, then grabbed me and shoved my head backwards, under the chilly water—and not once, but three times!

The average eight year old loves the water, but I was terrified of it: my mother had a cousin who'd drowned and thus, not wanting me to drown, had never let me near any sizable body of water. My kneejerk response to the assault and attempted drowning was to kick and flail wildly, splashing water out of the little tank. Brother Adams, who didn't seem like the type to harm a child, tried to calm me down, and I believe there were a few chuckles. He did steady me, and I survived—barely.

If somebody had told me you could get the same get-out-of-hell card with far less water at a Methodist church, my eventual destination, I'd have rushed straight into their arms. Once in a while, when I'm dabbing little drops of water on the forehead of an infant, or of a teenager or adult, I remember my baptism, with a mixture of gratitude and relief. If baptism is wedded to the deadly seriousness of following Jesus, then my brink-of-death dunking is strangely fitting. At the same time, I am awed by the gentler beauty of just a few drops, water enough, as full of the grace and power of God as a mighty flood.

Who would have guessed that, in this habit of violently casting children (and me in particular) into water, Brother Adams had compatriots all the way in South Carolina? We moved south, where there were even more Baptists. When I was in the fifth grade, some boys in the neighborhood invited me to a party at Lake Murray: lots of kids (who only now divulged that they were Baptists), games, hot dogs, Kool-Aid—all great fun.

But there was the lake. Kids kept urging me to jump in, but I kept my distance, manufacturing some flimsy excuse, probably that I had a cold (sniffle, sniffle, cough, cough . . .); how could I admit to the embarrassment of not knowing how to swim? Kids being kids, they persisted, pressured, cajoled, coaxed—and finally four of them forcibly hoisted my body into the air and threw me into the drink. Clearly I had underestimated how eager Baptists are to get you into the water.

Submerged, I lost all sense of which way was up, or down—and my gasp for air resulted in nothing but a billowing draught of murky lake water. I was sure I was drowning. But then a courageous Sunday School teacher leaped in and somehow wrestled my flailing self onto the shore—and it cost him a broken rib. So once again the Baptists nearly killed me, and simultaneously saved me.

The parabolic meaning of this event is pretty obvious. The Christian life is perilous; you find yourself in over your head. Walking on water (that over-the-top miracle Peter pulled off) isn't the best metaphor of the Christian life. Instead, following Jesus is like the disorientation, the desperation, loss of control and being seized unexpectedly that I experienced—or maybe I'm supposed to be the one to suffer some broken bones as I get close enough to save somebody who's similarly floundering.

Actually, the Baptist saving of my soul wasn't done yet. Fortunately Act Three involved not nearly so much water—only as much as can be measured in a grown man's tears. In sixth grade, I ventured into the building of the Baptists who tried to drown me. I was told to go to a boys' Sunday School class. The teacher was named Floyd Busby. He seemed to be at least 147 years old. He sported a flat top and spoke in a nasally voice. No one had trained him in hands-on, interactive, age-appropriate instructional techniques. And why did he keep coming back Sunday after

Struck from Behind

Sunday? We giggled and made fun of him behind his back—or more likely we only imagined we'd cloaked our snickering.

But I remember Mr. Busby vividly. One Sunday, while we were yawning and poking at each other, he launched into a long, seemingly endless reading from his tattered Bible. We barely noticed the topic, the arrest of Jesus, how he was ridiculed, mocked, and beaten, how he bore a cross up a hill, how his feet and hands were nailed into the wood. Then, to our surprise, there was a long silence. The whiny voice broke off. We looked up from our silliness. His head was hanging down. We wondered if he had died. But he wasn't dead. He was crying—and this was in the 1960s, when men just didn't cry. Somehow we resisted the temptation to laugh—which quickly subsided, for somehow we dimly realized we were in the presence of something holy. He restrained his sorrow and said to us, "Don't you boys see what they did to my Lord?"

I will never forget Mr. Busby's love for his Lord—and it was a seed that grew in the dark until I could say "our" Lord. Years later, I tried to look him up and thank him for teaching me. But it was in vain. He was not to be found. He gave of himself in teaching all those years with no feedback save the clamor of foolish, juvenile boys to get out of his room as quickly as possible.

I understand now that these Southern Baptists were "fundamentalist" in outlook. I suppose I've known my share of severe fundamentalists, those who turn the Bible into a weapon, who can smile sweetly and say "Jesus" and "Lord" while harboring a steely narrowness in their hearts. I have also known my share of warm-hearted fundamentalists, who adore the Bible too much to question it, who love Jesus enough to want everybody to be holy, who sacrifice plenty out of simple devotion to Jesus. My grandparents were such fundamentalists, and as I grow old I continue to be blessed by a few others.

I was scared of the preachers I heard, and yet somehow I became one, and have warm memories of church. I can chalk it up to a curious custom: churches in every place insist that we sing together, no matter the quality. My favorite hymns, to this day, I learned before elementary school. I recall raising my voice with the congregation as we sang "Holy, Holy, Holy," probably because the lyrics were easy and repetitive, or the chord structure touched something deep within—or perhaps it was the enthusiastic singing of somebody in a pew cattycorner to me, which I noticed. My sister was in some little girls' choir: why do I recall sitting in the hallway, with my mother, waiting for rehearsal to end? The girls broke into a lovely harmony (probably the first they'd ever tried, given their age) on "Fairest Lord Jesus." Beautiful savior indeed.

Jesus Said, Follow Me

God was a covert yet sustaining presence through my elementary, junior high, and high school years. My life was about sports, girls, school, TV. My attentiveness to God was all but nonexistent—and so can only echo Jacob's discovery at Bethel: "Surely the Lord was in this place, but I did not know it" (Gen 28:16).

Off to college I went, never for a fleeting moment entertaining the questions I've asked my own children and church folk for decades now: What is God calling you to do? Are prayers, Bible study, worship and service part of your routine? I didn't avoid church and such things; they never crossed my mind.

But God's pursuit of me was gathering a little momentum. Some guys I knew, including my closest childhood friend and then college roommate, Carl, were heavily involved at a church near campus. They didn't speak of the church by its name—Trinity Episcopal. What they were giddy about was a gathering of college kids called "Team," a Young Life-ish time of singing, games, prayer and a message led by a young minister named John Yates, who would eventually become the rector of the lovely Episcopal congregation in Falls Church, Virginia—notorious for their long-running feud with the diocese over homosexuality (or scriptural authority, depending on your viewpoint on such matters).

But I had not yet met John, didn't know what an Episcopalian was, and didn't care to find out what this "Team" was all about. Guys kept inviting me, but I just didn't care enough to drive a few blocks, get free food, play volleyball, and sing a few songs. But they were persistent—like those Baptists flinging me into Lake Murray. Their diligence saved me. I'm reminded of that wonderful anecdote from Mark 2, where a paralytic is hauled to Jesus by four men. Undeterred by obstacles, they hoisted the paralytic up on the roof, dug through the thatched ceiling, and lowered him into the room where Jesus was. What does Mark tell us? "When Jesus saw their faith, he said to the paralytic, 'Your sins are forgiven' " (Mark 2:5). *Their* faith: whether the paralytic had faith or not we do not know; but it was their faith that saved him. I had no faith when their nagging got me to Team. Their faith saved me.

Struck from Behind

I caved in and said I would go—just once. I could not have felt more uncomfortable. People carrying Bibles bound in hippie covers, singing songs I'd never heard, long stretches of time with our eyes shut, with an occasional guy or gal voicing some seemingly trivial concern to God: "Help me on my calculus exam" or "Keep us safe as we drive to the beach tomorrow" or "I praise you for getting me a parking place downtown."

But as the evening moved along, I warmed up to being there—and why? In a more pious tale, I would have been moved by the pastor's message, or haunted by God into a swooning conversion. But no: as I surveyed the room, I noticed a surprising number of great-looking women. I decided I'd be quite clever and come back to get to know a few if possible, although I wondered if I could pull off the façade of appearing to be sufficiently spiritual.

And so I did. I was awkward socially so I stumbled a few times, spent some fun evenings with a couple of them, and then fell in love with one who broke my heart. But no matter: I kept showing up. I came to enjoy the music, and started paying attention to the messages, although I just couldn't get the hang of prayer. I kept hearing pitches about joining a small group, that big group is fun but the real wonder is in these smaller Bible study/prayer conclaves that met on yet another evening each week. *Another evening? Are you kidding? You're lucky to have me here at all! No way will I ever go to a small group*—where I would be even more uncomfortable, less able to hide. And the groups are either all men or all women? *How would I meet chicks at an all men's group?*

In the Bible, God speaks to people through dreams. I'm never sure what to make of that, as my dreams are the typical kinds psychologists understand: running late for an exam, realizing you are unclothed in public, a house burning down, being chased. A dream seems like a dicey medium for God to use to speak to somebody, as you forget your dreams so easily, or can't interpret them beyond the admission of craziness dancing in your head through the night.

And yet I am sure God spoke to me, and saved me, through a dream. One night, during this time I'd sworn I would never ever go to a Bible study group, I had an extraordinarily vivid dream—the kind that feels more palpably real than the world you wake up to, the kind you recall later and say "I'd have sworn that really happened." In this quite solid dream, Jesus (how did I know who it was?) looked straight at me, and said two simple words: "Follow me."

I woke suddenly, raised up in the bed and looked around the corner to see where he'd gone. I made some coffee, and tried to forget the dream in the busyness of the day, but could not. I remembered that one of those Bible study groups was supposed to meet that very evening. To go or not to go? All day long I thought I'd go, felt sure I wouldn't, knew I had to.

Gingerly I knocked on the door, wary of too much pious hospitality. I was greeted warmly but not too warmly (thankfully), grabbed a Coke, ate some chips, made small talk—and then it was time to begin. Jim Tasker, a lovely Australian who would become a dear friend in the very near future, opened his Bible and said "This evening we will want to look at Matthew, chapter 4, verse 19. 'Jesus said to them, Follow me . . .' "

What did he say? He Jim Tasker? He Jesus? Follow me? I was seized by a dizzy confusion, or a gasping wonder. I cannot recall anything else that was said that evening. But my world shifted on its axis. From that moment on, I have tried, however laughably and wretchedly, to make my life an answer to that dream, to the words Peter, Andrew, James, and John heard by the sea back in the first century from that most beautiful voice that ever spoke, the voice of the one who loved me enough to visit me uninvited during the night: "Follow me."

The Second Coming

But I was still a mess, determined to follow Jesus, but I did so in a gelatinous, malformed kind of way. I was plagued by ignorance, susceptible to the occasionally questionable beliefs of whatever Christians I happened to run into who were good to me. I knew a handful of believers for whom Hal Lindsey's *Late Great Planet Earth* was virtually a second Bible. They pounded into me not a belief but rather a fear that Jesus really might return soon. I worried a little, aware I was too green and too inexpert at faith to be one caught up into the clouds. At the same time, I suspected all this apocalyptic fantasy was ridiculous, as did my closest friends—but who could be sure?

Four of us were together at dinner on September 1, 1975. I know the date precisely because followers of Lindsey and his tribe had latched onto the idea that Jesus would return that August (acknowledging with thin humility that we cannot know the *exact* date)—which was now past. I announced, "Well, I guess Jesus didn't come back after all." My smart-alecky friend across the table replied, "Yeah? How would you know?"

Struck from Behind

Har har—but a good point. If Jesus returned to take the faithful home, we lacked proper credentials.

So we decided to conduct a little test. Whom did we know who would be most likely to have been taken up? We agreed on a lovely, very holy soprano we knew named Glo—and we actually hadn't seen her for a couple of weeks . . . We drove to her house. Her car was in the driveway. *Good, she's home.* We went to the door, and heard music playing on the stereo inside. *Of course, she's listening to music.* One of us mashed the doorbell, and we waited—and waited. Another knocked loudly with his knuckles—and still nothing. Silently, we turned to walk back to the car. Just as I reached out to open the passenger door, a voice pierced the quiet: "Hey, guys!" She'd been out in the back yard.

Funny thing is, three of the four of us wound up as ordained clergy. What were we thinking in that awkward gap between the doorbell and her calling out to us? Little wonder that, once I got to seminary, I gulped down real scholarship on the book of Revelation, apocalyptic, and the "end times" (or, to use the big word I learned and loved, "eschatology").

In fact, my faith trek has always involved trying to use my native smartness not only to know more about God and things religious, but also to secure my place among other believers. Trying to sort out where I belonged, I experimented with a brief stint as an apologist, the defender of the faith, the intellectual counter to the secular heresies of science and biblical scholarship. I could parrot the arguments of Josh McDowell, Henry Morris, and John Warwick Montgomery and prove the Gospels were factually accurate and Jesus really did rise from the dead. I tried my best to strike a heroic pose for my intellectually nervous college friends clinging to literal faith.

But this little foray lasted maybe three months. Lovely girls in the group sighed and smiled while I bravely stood up for the Lord, but the enterprise was self-defeating, and didn't suit my preternatural habits of being critical and a malcontent when it comes to settled thought. Yet, my life as a religious egghead had begun. I took religion courses, and was enraptured by Professor Don Jones, who cockily took on southern fundamentalists with an unforgettable opening salvo in lecture number one: "Now if you disagree with me, that's fine; if you want to be wrong, that's your business." He exposed historical flaws in the Gospels, unveiled divergent yet early manuscript readings of pet passages, and drove the Southern Baptists in the crowd to the brink of rage.

I was hooked, and somehow have never quite grasped what all the pious fuss has been about. Flaws in scripture? Mistakes of historical memory? Accounts that disagree? What would one expect from documents surviving over two thousand years? And blemishes and goofs? I was myself a walking jumble of blemishes and goofs, so such scriptures and beliefs suited me. It took me a while to be able to articulate all this, but the heart of the gospel is that the Word became flesh and dwelt among us. God entered into this mortal coil and became as pierceable, grievable, misunderstandable, and rejectable as I find myself to be. I like that. I want flawed scriptures, and a flawed church—and have been blessed with both, and contributed my fair share to the flawedness.

Frankly, a Christianity that panics or withers in the face of criticism isn't a sound enough faith to bank my life upon. Christopher Lasch was onto something when he wrote,

> It is only by subjecting our preferences to the test of debate that we come to understand what we know and what we still need to learn. Until we have to defend our opinions in public, they remain mere opinions, half-formed convictions based on random impressions and unexamined assumptions.[1]

For me it isn't that we will always marshal the facts and reasoning and defeat our foes; I'm okay with losing. The gospel is far larger than a mere fact, the story more compelling than a falsity here or there, the truth about God eluding any interpretive framework. It is the "love that moves the stars" (Dante's lovely phrase) enveloping all of history, and my life, sweeping us along an irresistible tide toward the good end we all have a hankering for.

Why Seminary?

For the life of me I cannot recall what made me start thinking about seminary. Vaguely I recall talking with a religion professor, who suggested the idea—not as a pathway into ministry, but as the middle step toward a PhD in religion. He had one, he regarded me as a groupie—and aren't all of us delighted (or validated) when the young want to take up our line of work?

I've discovered over the years quite a few people who *nearly* went to seminary. Conversations with them are always intriguing. Some peeked in

---

1. Christopher Lasch, *Revolt of the Elites and the Betrayal of Democracy* (New York: Norton, 1995), 170.

the window of ministry, felt overwhelmed, and now spend their days with a breezy sense of relief that they didn't walk in. Others express a kind of longing regret over what might have been. I find myself suggesting seminary to all kinds of people, and not merely to those who show "promise," largely because I showed no promise. My hunch is that if you grapple however briefly with the possibility of a life in full-time ministry, your perspectives on the life of faith, and service of God, are indelibly altered. Most folks I've known who *almost* went to seminary are gentle with and appreciative of those of us who took the plunge.

Why did I go? I had abandoned physics, hadn't piled up quite enough pre-med prerequisites (and to this day blanche at the sight of blood), and forgot to sign up for the LSAT. Maybe this new passion for things religious should be pursued. If I had a call from God, it flitted about in some subterranean cavern in my soul, unnoticed. Become a minister? I only knew one, his style would never be mine—and anyhow, he'd moved to Pennsylvania. Become a minister and have a romantic life? I found pretty quickly, even thinking of enrolling in seminary, that the women I fancied dating would turn chilly at the mention of divinity school, and then women who warmed to the idea were women to whom I didn't warm.

I fished around to learn about schools. My academic mentors pressed me toward Yale, Princeton, Duke; my religious friends pushed me toward Gordon-Conwell, or a new startup called Trinity Evangelical Divinity School. I cannot sort out why I chose Duke, except that my close friend Tom was going there, and I'd been a fan of their basketball team in the 1960s. Basketball would prove to be a happy circumstance, as Duke's resurgence to the top of the NCAA ranks began with the 1978 Final Four run in my second year of div school.

What a crucial choice that was: to have gone to Gordon-Conwell, I often think, would have helped me have a simpler, more zealous faith—but would that really have suited who I am? My spiritual life probably would have been more strongly constructed, or at least more rapidly sure of itself—but then perhaps not. I had no calling, and was wobbly in my sense of believing. A call can be like that, for those who'll wind up among the clergy but also for any Christian hoping to fulfill whatever calling God has in store: a gnarl of dreams, chance meetings, bits of wisdom, some dumb advice, wishes, stumbles—and you have to scramble out of the thicket somehow, and when you're back on your feet, that's your call.

Following Jesus can be costly. No, that's incorrect: following Jesus *is* costly. We prefer to say "can be," as it feels safer, less threatening, and allow us to pick and choose ways of following that don't cost so much. But I have always understood quite clearly the cost, even the heartache of those bizarre things Jesus said that bug most people—about his setting father against son, or the little discussed fact that when James and John were invited by Jesus to follow, they left not only their nets but also their father Zebedee.

When I began to flirt with the idea of seminary or maybe even ministry, I told my father. He's never been a church guy at all. A classic child of the Depression, focused on the power of money to rise up to a better life and stave off disaster, he thought I would follow in his footsteps, in engineering, or at least do something with upward mobility, societal respect, and the prospects of financial security and comfort. I shall never forget his reaction—although could I really read his emotions behind the words? He said to me, quite clearly, "Son, you have the chance to be somebody. Don't waste it."

But what did he mean? For years I let that percolate in my gut, and parsed it as if he regarded ministry as a waste. I even quoted this moment (and wish I hadn't) in a few sermons, and in a couple of graduation speeches I made. You can imagine: do what you are called to do, even if those around you think you're crazy—even if it's your father. I felt the sanctifying support of St. Francis, who famously mortified his father Pietro Bernardone, and wound up shedding everything his father had ever given him, including the clothes off his back, in order to become nothing less than a saint. The specter of Pietro never again speaking to his son, and even spitting in his direction when they would happen upon one another, was something I could understand, and perhaps, in some dark corner of my hidden self, even relish.

But was that what my father intended? We hear others, and especially parents, or spouses, or our own children, in such convoluted ways, interjecting our own craziness. Perhaps he simply was issuing a very apropos warning, or even dispensing sheer wisdom—the very kind of counsel we should all give one another. Perhaps this was what Jesus intended when he invited fishermen to drop their nets or for Zaccheus to climb down from the sycamore tree, or when he wrote in the sand in front of the woman caught in adultery. *You have the chance to be somebody. Don't waste it.*

Chapter 9

Backing Into Ministry
Living in the Church

To SAY THAT ON the day I enrolled at Duke Divinity School I'd heard a call to ministry would be an exaggeration of what was going on inside my head. God, what little I could apprehend of God, held considerable allure, certainly as a topic for thought, and secretly as a more personal obsession. If you asked me on day one what job I might hold, I guess I'd answer that I might be a teacher or a counselor, fascinated as I was with the field of psychology (or perhaps with the thicket of twisted feelings and confusion in my own head). In retrospect, I believe I was in flight from the trajectory my dad or my chemistry teachers might have projected for me. I've always had a notorious inclination throughout my life to attempt things I cannot possibly do well: trying out for varsity sports with my short, skinny, unathletic frame, asking the head cheerleader out for a date, picking up golf clubs, or later in life devising ways to reform my entire denomination.

My native intelligence, assessed by standardized tests, suggested I should not venture far from zones involving math and science. Just being a bright person rendered me an unlikely candidate: did I laugh or shudder at my twentieth high school reunion when a classmate, shocked to hear I had gone into the ministry, employed a puzzled tone of disappointment when he said, "But you were so smart"? Smart, maybe, but socially inept, and a total chicken in public settings.

I am absolutely certain any capacity I might have to be a preacher is a humbling, miraculous gift, not some exercise of my natural abilities. I can prove it: as a senior in college, I'd gotten to be part of the leadership team of Team, that Young-Lifey group that actually saved my life, not because I exhibited any leadership traits, but because I knew how to play the piano. John Yates, the pastor, had left, and things weren't going so smoothly with his successor (named John Wesley, oddly enough to me now that I'm Methodist). We met, and decided one of the student leaders should address the group to bolster morale. Who should it be? Some jokester said "Hey, how about James?"—and the group fell into a fit of giggles.

I was not hurt in the least. I was the last person who could or would stand in front of anybody to say anything at all. This is one of the reasons to this day I am not unabashedly fond of those spiritual gifts inventories churches offer, which suggest that you look to the way you are made, what you're good at, your inherent or accrued abilities, and that is what you use to serve God. With this common approach, accountants and bankers serve on finance committees, schoolteachers and ex-professors teach, those who love travel venture out on mission junkets, seamstresses knit prayer shawls.

But God asked stuttering Moses to talk, aged Abraham to father children, Amos the herdsman to be a prophet, Galilean fishermen to evangelize, the stylish Francis to touch lepers outside Assisi, and even a nobody timid science junkie like me to be of all things a preacher. If so, then doesn't God call all of us out of our comfort zones, out of the box of what we already know we can manage, into situations of inability and discomfort? Isn't this so we will depend upon God, so we stretch into the new creatures God is fashioning, so we even embrace defeat as a lovely lesson in the adventure of faith? We shrink back from the possibility of failure or awkwardness—but doesn't God invite us to follow him and fail, and even be shattered on the altar of offering self in total abandon to the God who seems to enjoy putting failure and ineptness to good use?

Father Murphy

My first day at seminary was my luckiest. As an incredibly naïve twenty-year-old numb with confusion over how to negotiate class selection or how simply to be among students I assumed would be far holier than myself, I literally crashed into a tall, gangly professor in the hallway as we both turned a corner. He roared with laughter, clutched my hand, and announced himself as Father Roland Murphy—and invited me into his office. Soon he was my advisor, and teacher, as I signed up for every course of his that would fit my schedule.

Struck from Behind

Over time he hired me as a research assistant, as a teaching assistant, and as editor for some of his voluminous publishing endeavors. He was what academics call my "Doktor Vater" (as it suits the vanity of eggheads when foreign phrases pass from their lips), directing my PhD work. Until his death, he was my mentor, sage, and friend. Mostly, for me, he really was "Father Murphy," very much a father figure in my life. No one called him Dr. Murphy. No one called him Professor Murphy. And no one called him Roland, although he would not have minded. We called him *Father* Murphy. Being Protestants, I think we relished the idea of having a Father.

He loomed—at 6'7" or maybe more. When my roommates and I had him over for dinner, he knocked over a bottle of wine trying to jam his long legs under our table. And yet from his height he curved downward to

us in class, almost as if God's accommodation to us mortals was imprinted on his posture. His hands were long; his spindly fingers pecked out his work on an old manual typewriter. He handwrote much, despite what he called "this damned palsy"—including the last note I got, whose legible sections detailed his illnesses and his pending writing projects, with a P.S. that read, "At least I don't have Alzheimer's yet."

All students recall him ranging about the front of the room, Bible in hand, voice booming, boring into some passage like a miner chipping stone away to find diamonds. He never stood still. Occasionally he would smash into the blackboard, erasers tumbling in a cloud of dust. Once he spun on a remark made on the other side of the room, and his Bible flew from his hand, as if thrown at the hapless student.

His face (which I jokingly told him reminded me of that El Greco version of St. Jerome as a cardinal, which hung in his office and graced the cover of the *Jerome Biblical Commentary*—which he edited!) was effusively expressive, deploying an assortment of grimaces, scowls, smirks, grins, raised eyebrows. From behind that face came not just words but other sounds, gutturals, too deep for mere words: *Ha!!* or *Huummm?. . .* or a growling *Ugghhh . . .*, pained evocations from within, if you showed lack of comprehension, but then the rewarding *Ummmm*, like a bear having swallowed a delicious piece of meat, should you utter something wise. The most brilliant student was humbled, the appetite whetted; the slower students were always encouraged.

We who studied with him do not remember the precise points that he made in his lectures, but his palpable, giddy excitement over an open Bible was contagious. He was one of the world's premier scholars, but he wore his extensive learning lightly, and was modest about honor and acclaim. Once I stepped into his office, sat down, and said, "Tell me about this George Washington Ivey chair" (one of the most prestigious honors at the university just awarded him)—and he said, "Well, look under your behind, you're sitting on it." At his insistence, I always sat in the prestigious chair, as did countless students who discovered to their surprise that this bountifully productive writer was always interruptable. He would look up from that typewriter mid-peck and talk with you for as long as was needed, and then plunge back into his work unflustered. Of course, were it time for his daily swim, the interruptor got to walk with him to the pool.

Father Murphy taught the Wisdom books of the Bible. He not only knew a lot about wisdom; he was wise, perhaps the wisest person I have ever known. I did not make any important life decisions without consulting him. To this day, when I feel that gaping hole of uncertainty, that hunger for some perspective or somebody to tell me the truth, God's truth for me, I miss him terribly.

He was revered by scholars all over the world, and was even more beloved by elderly Catholic ladies I have met in places like Rock Hill, Pennsylvania and Wisconsin. He once told me he decided to be a priest when he was a little boy. To prepare himself, he learned French, Spanish, German, Portuguese, Arabic, Hebrew, Italian, and a few other languages so he could hear confession from any person who happened to come along. His professors steered this brilliant young man toward the study of Bible, where he proved to be a valiant pioneer, opening the windows of the Catholic church to the strange world of the scriptures.

Struck from Behind

Father Murphy's contributions to Catholicism were matched by his ecumenical achievements. Without treating it like a big deal, he became the first Catholic faculty member at Methodist Duke Divinity School, and brokered countless conversations among Christians of all persuasions, helping them to understand one another. My lifelong delights in ecumenism, both in thought and in friendships with others, should be chalked up to his example.

Father Murphy died with considerable panache, exquisite timing: one day past his own eighty-fifth birthday, he died on what Roman Catholics observe as the Feast Day of Elijah—liturgically fitting for a professor of Old Testament who was also of the Carmelite order, those quirky Catholics devoted to Elijah! I imagined him being swept up into the heavens on a chariot to meet St. Francis, those little old ladies who adored him, his own mother, and brother, St. Jerome, and Elijah himself.

For Father Murphy, the scriptures have a scholarly usefulness, but also a pastoral function that is all grace, giving shape, hope, and expression to a buoyant sense of the holy. I was to serve as his teaching assistant for a course on the Psalms. I popped by his office three months before the class commenced to see what he would recommend I read to be on top of things. His norm with other courses had been to rattle off the titles of a dozen or two dozen books, mostly in German, huge, thick tomes with miniscule fonts, towering exhibitions of scholarly complexity. But he shocked me, and assigned what I thought would be easy: "Pray" (not "read," but "pray") "one Psalm each morning, and one each evening." That's it? The possibilities of more sleep, and more tennis, opened up in my relieved mind.

But that very day I left his office to visit my friend Thaniel, who had been admitted to Duke Medical Center in her flagging battle against cystic fibrosis. She kindly asked me what route I took to her hospital room, and if it was out of the way. I explained that I normally cut through the hospital on the way from my apartment to the seminary, and vice versa on the way home in the evening. She said, "I have a huge favor to ask."

"Anything," I replied. She requested: "If you can, when you come and go in the morning and evening, stop by my room and read a Psalm, one in the morning, and one in the evening, even after I seem too discombobulated or incoherent to understand or interact." I pondered this startling request, and my suspicions rose, so I asked, "Are you in cahoots with Father Murphy?" She looked back blankly.

And so I learned the Psalms, those ancient articulations of praise, grief, confession, gratitude, and hope, not in the seminary classroom, but in a hospital room with a young friend who would not live long enough to get through all 150 Psalms. I continued the discipline after her funeral, and through much of my life.

Living Inside the Church

So the balance of what I recall about God in this narrative of my life of faith involves the things I've experienced and done as a pastor. Don't worry, reader: this won't devolve into a "my life in ministry" saga. It's fascinating to me, and I've been grateful for most (but far from all) that has transpired. But it's another book I likely will never write: too dull, too many personal stories involving people who've trusted my confidentiality, too much "here's how ministry used to be."

I backed into this work. I actually finished divinity school, and served as a full-time pastor for some time, before I realized I was called into the ministry. After seminary, and at the midway point in my PhD work, I dreamed of a life in academics. Then one night I got a phone call, asking if I could fill a spot at a little country church. I didn't want to and said no, twice actually. When I was phoned a third time, inexplicably I said *Yes*, thinking I would stay a year. As of this writing, I've stayed thirty-two years in this befuddling but marvelous work.

Through my experience in the life of the church, paired with ongoing theological study and reflection, I have learned more and more about God, and more and more of what I don't yet know about God. I have refined a few things in my mind, like the threeness that is God, what we believe about the saving action of Jesus, and our relationship to other religions, and why and how these things matter for real people in and out of the church.

What I would share is this: if you are reading something like this theological memoir, you must be interested in God, and in the web of connections with God that a life might inhabit. My staggering privilege as a pastor is to hear one person's story, and then another and another. I get to sit in front of the front row in worship and see the faces of people singing, praying, seeking, crying, napping, laughing, grimacing.

I'm paid to read theology, Greek New Testament and Hebrew Bible, and to think of those things when I read the paper or hang out with folks at a party. I'm paid to go into those sacred zones in hospitals, and get to be an honorary, if temporary family member. I witness up close the darkest days, which often are also the days in which we all rise to our greatest nobility, at the thinnest possible place where God is palpably present, helpful, both strangely absent and surely there, and surprisingly comforting. I get to talk about God right out in the open, so people might notice in real time some of the things mentioned in this memoir that I've only recognized in retrospect.

I've also learned a lot about God, and God's people. I have found church people (despite the occasional grouser who firmly believes God placed him on earth to make my life miserable) to be implacably patient. Most, though not all, have been merciful to me when I didn't know what I was doing (and that was the first time I climbed into a pulpit, but also just last Sunday; my first hospital visit but then actually all of them; my first committee meeting and all the rest), when I was tone deaf to their hurts or forgot their names, and when I made mistakes. Good Lord, when I think of my missteps I am so very grateful I did not become a neurosurgeon, for my errors seem not to have been fatal to too many people.

Never, not even once, have I pretended to be especially holy or flawless; I am open about the broken humanity that is mine, and ours. Sometimes I hide my real hurts and fears. Clergy do this, and feel a bit put upon, thinking it is due to some vocational pressure. But church folks do this all the time, and I understand their bent to privacy, but then also the chilly isolation. Church cannot possibly be as isolating as consumer society.

I always plead with people to give a church a chance, especially a little one that doesn't seem to hold much promise in today's scramble for the large, full-service megachurches I've pastored lately. When I heard about my first pastoral location, I found a map, which was detailed but not detailed enough to display the road on which my ministerial work would begin (and where I would live five years of my life). I jumped in the car and drove two hours, through and then out of the little town nearby, down a road with no signage, cutting through the woods—and then there was the church, pretty enough but lonely, with a house that would be my home perched next door. A cemetery stretched along the other side of the road. A city boy, unmarried, vulnerable to bouts of dark loneliness, leaving the headiness of Duke University: I put the car in park, laid my head on the steering wheel, cried for longer than I care to admit, and tried to figure out how to back out of my commitment.

But how wrong I was. The church family that was and still is Wesley Chapel United Methodist Church proved to be a welcoming womb of love and fun, carrying me when I was clueless (which was most days). Quite effortlessly they included me in daily life as if I'd grown up there. I did the unimaginable (for me): I grew vegetables, and then canned them; I hunted, and killed a buck my first day up in a tree; I went to the slaughtering of a hog, and to corn-shuckings. Calvin Barringer picked me up one morning and drove toward the middle of nowhere. I asked where we were headed, and he replied, "Rattlesnake hunting!" I gulped, and assured him, "Calvin, I don't want to find them." We worshiped, prayed, studied the Bible, taught children, buried the dead, married the young—and I would defy any megachurch to match that congregation's faith, hope, and love.

I've spoken in chapter 4 about the way they were a bit over-zealous to get me married. When I did marry they all came to the wedding in the church I would later pastor, and loved and welcomed Lisa as if she were an angel alighting in their midst. On our last Sunday, we all cried, and they gave us the best parting gift ever: a quilt, which had been stitched by every woman in that parish. Each square in the quilt was a memory of something I'd said in a sermon, or that buck I'd killed, or the vegetables I'd grown, or the early days of my courting Lisa, things we'd shared as a church family. That quilt is the perfect emblem of this memoir: we are wrapped and warmed by the memories of this good life together, and that snuggled comfort is the very presence of God.

Can the Clergy Be Saved?

Lisa and I married, and it seemed to be time for new work. A well-meaning District Superintendent, one of the bishop's henchmen charged with the deployment of clergy, put his arm around me, and told me "The Plaza church has lots of problems; you'll be perfect for it." His unintended punchline elicited not so much a chuckle as a shiver. He was right, about the church's problems that is, though not about my perfection for the task. We pulled up with our U-Haul of family belongings, and a man I did not know met me in the driveway, not to help ferry stuff into the house, but to report somebody had died and I needed to do something, and now. That afternoon the church treasurer came by and laid out the bleakest possible financial scenario, which in the business world would have counted for worse than bankruptcy. Then a board meeting that night: an evidently long-standing argument re-erupted between two leaders, who growled curse words at one another until the tall one threw his pencil at the stocky one and stormed out of the room. *What the . . .?* Weren't church folk obligated to at least pretend to be loving or minimally polite?

The church's membership had been shrinking for two decades. There wasn't even a sign telling passersby the building was in fact a church—and I had a few doubts myself. Year one was a grueling tug-of-war, me on one side, the rest of the crowd on the other, and I was only holding my own because of sheer dint of will, and the fact that my life was on the line in a way theirs wasn't. I asked the bishop for a new job, but he didn't have one for me. I wasn't sure I could stay one more week.

But somehow I stayed five years, and when the time came to leave, we cried—yes, *we* cried, I did, my family did, and the guys who cursed at one another did as well. Churches and church people can surprise you if you stick with them. I think during those days I read Scott Peck's anecdote of the woman who was unhappy in her marriage: when he asked why she stayed, she said "For the friction."[1] Indeed. Friction provides considerable drama, so you know you're alive. Yet friction also produces some warmth when it's cold. And friction polishes. I think I learned at Plaza that if you stick with the friction, and gamely try to love anyhow, you get polished; rough edges get smoothed out so that, if only because you hang in there, you actually mirror the heart of God to the world.

One's "church home" can be homely, or worse. But instead of fleeing the place, maybe we stay, look around the room, and acknowledge that all churches and all of us who occupy them are adroit copycats of those biblical families and clumps of apostles: Jacob's dysfunctional family (or David's), or those puckish disciples, baffled and inept, not shying away from chicanery and violence, an embarrassment to the God trying to use them. The scriptures seem to embrace us in our kookiness; precisely because we ourselves are so homely, we're actually right at home in a homely church.

I also skim a little over my life as a minister in this memoir because of the peculiar fact that every Christian is called by God to ministry, to vocation. I think some in my extended family have harbored some unexplainable pride in having one among all the cousins who was called by God—but God calls all of them too. God has big plans, enormous assignments, a life work for each one of us. The unordained aren't sequestered from that any more than I am.

If anything they are less safe. Or at least, I feel sure I would have been less safe from myself all these years had I not been in ordained ministry.

---

1. Scott Peck, *A World Waiting to be Born* (New York: Bantam, 1993), 105.

Lots of clergy complain that they live in a glass house, that people have unreasonable expectations that they will be pious and exemplary. I never complain: I think the pressure to be good has helped me to be good, or at least better. God knows what trouble I'd have gotten myself into without it.

When I look into my gut I do not find the slightest trace of natural piety, and at the same time I do see a seething cauldron of impulses that could at any moment be my undoing. My work has kept a lot of that in check, or at least unexpressed. I find myself to be quite fond of what Barnaby Gaitlin said in Anne Tyler's novel, *A Patchwork Planet*: "Someday I should get credit for all the things I don't say," or do for that matter.[2] I know lots of clergy misbehave, and I know for certain I am capable of all sorts of dastardly deeds. For me, being known publicly as Reverend has helped me to be good—and it seems the church might figure out how to do that same favor for everybody in the church. Maybe church mission statements might add something like "We will help one another not to behave badly."

I do not know if I would be very prayerful if I didn't have to be prayerful professionally. I am not sure I would be an avid Bible reader if it were not a requirement for me to earn a living. I'm grateful. Those prayers I've had to pray, and the Bible study I've been forced to do, have helped me immensely. Karl Barth once asked (and all clergy in humility resonate to his question), "Can a minister be saved?" His clever, comforting reply? "With men this is impossible; but with God all things *are* possible."[3] I'm counting on God's possibility.

And finally, I'm reluctantly drawn to another wry observation from Barth—that the clergy might be "hopeful but not happy."[4] Have I been happy as a minister? I'm unsure of the answer, or even if it is the right question. Happy? Enormously, but then for longer stretches than I care to admit even to myself, not very. But then yesterday was a wonderful, profoundly meaningful day. I cannot in retrospect imagine another life. Living in the church, with the people of God, sharing their most harrowing and joyful moments, studying the things of God, has been more of a privilege than somebody like me could ever dare to ask for.

And yet I wish I'd done more, or differently. I am saddened by failures, or how little we've gotten done, or that I didn't make more of a difference. Achievements in working life, whether in ordained ministry or at

2. Anne Tyler, *A Patchwork Planet* (New York: Ballantine, 1999), 285.

3. Karl Barth, *The Word of God and the Word of Man*, trans. Douglas Horton (Gloucester: Smith, 1978), 126.

4. Ibid., 183.

the bank or law office or in agriculture or plumbing, do not entirely banish sorrow in the rest of life, although it helps, which might explain why so many people get addicted to their work. And perhaps it is a humbling aspect of our fallen nature that we are saddled with both high expectations and inevitable disappointments. Because of this, we aim higher, and realize our dependence upon grace.

I wonder if Barth is right, and that happiness *is* more elusive for the clergy. I resonate to one of Graham Greene's typically wise reflections:

> Despair is the price one pays for setting oneself an impossible aim. It is . . . the unforgivable sin, but it is a sin the corrupt or evil man never practices. He always has hope . . . Only the man of goodwill carries always in his heart this capacity for damnation.[5]

Between happiness and damnation there stretches a dizzying spread of possibilities and happenings, feelings and realities. In between, I find that I do believe. The faith I have is nothing I mustered, but is itself the most precious gift of a God who for reasons inexplicable wanted to be intimate with me.

---

5. Graham Greene, *The Heart of the Matter* (New York: Penguin, 1948), 50.

Chapter 10

Knives, Trains, Baby Shoes
Gifts Received & Given

IF LIFE IS A gift, if God resides in our memory as an exquisite gift waiting to be opened, then the gifts we have given and received, the presents
we wrapped carefully or tore into with gusto might give us clues that will
reveal what is in God's heart, like generosity, grace, and goodness. I know
that, for me, when I contemplate moments gifts were given and received,
this endeavor cultivates in my soul holy dispositions toward my own past,
like gratitude, humility, wonder and love.

Admittedly we get confused by gift-giving, and gift-receiving.
Surely Jesus is perplexed when we pervert Advent and Christmas into a
big birthday party whose guest of honor appears to be . . . us, a shopping
and gifting frenzy, the zenith of consumer fantasy. And at Thanksgiving
we gorge ourselves in order to express—gratitude for God's gifts? Wasn't
Niebuhr right when he thundered that Thanksgiving as practiced in
America is little more than "self-righteous bunk," when we congratulate
the Almighty on his "most excellent coworkers—ourselves"?[1] That there
is a counterfeit kind of gifting sets into bold relief the real thing, which
mirrors God's grace quite beautifully.

I tried to run a little inventory on the presents I've been given, as
a boy at Christmas, on birthdays, Valentine's Day, anniversaries, and the
occasional random surprise—and find myself embarrassed that I cannot
now recall much of what I received. Giving is such an in-the-moment

1. Reinhold Niebuhr, *Leaves from the Notebook of a Tamed Cynic* (New York:
Harper & Row, 1929), 58.

thing; I've always enjoyed the anticipation, and the titillating moment of ripping the paper and lifting the lid from the box more than handling what's actually inside. And at the end of the day, when I have gotten whatever it is I have gotten, what I have really received (in overwrought and overly expensive, or slick and clever, or fumbling and misdirected ways) is love, or at least kind regard.

When I give gifts (and I take inordinate pride in finding just the right gift, and even being known as a terrific giver of gifts), what I am really striving to achieve is that the receiver, the opener, the beloved will feel beloved, opened up somehow, and received. God, the best of all givers, must have similar intent, making the sun shine, causing gravity to keep working, giving us little rays of hope in the guise of a child's smile or the taste of a strawberry, drawing our attention to a steeple or a leather-bound Bible on the coffee table, all in the hopes we will see ourselves as those given to, embraced, opened to the marvel of God's good world.

And I wonder if God is like me, far more comfortable giving than receiving. God gives; God is the ultimate giver. God can't need a thing, right? And yet, God must long to be the receiver of our giving, of our love. Although our giving to God may be like a child coloring a stick figure to present to mommy, or like that lame gift you bought your dad when you had no clue what somebody his age could possibly want but you bought something anyhow, God loves whatever we give, and knows how to receive with perfect, holy gratitude.

So let me share with you about a train, a rug, a bike, a couple of knives, the dumbest gift I ever got, and my kids' favorite custom for my birthday, and how God was mystically and quite vividly present, and how all of this has helped me welcome God's love, and to learn ways to love God and the people God loves.

Carry This in Your Pocket

The best gift I ever received was something I never wanted. A few days before I finished my twelfth and final year as pastor of a church I had loved deeply, the congregation's lay leader shuffled into my office. Nobody bothered to vote him in as lay leader. He just *was* the leader of the laity, the godfather of a sprawling church family united largely by their love for this giant of a man. James Alexander had turned eighty-nine. He carried himself as if whole centuries were draped over his shoulders. Wise, solid, very Southern, with a gravelly voice and surprisingly undiminished physical vigor, he wore overalls in a pretty dressy community.

We were awestruck by his evident holiness, not that smug, sanitized kind of holiness, but an earthy, calloused, believable holiness. He visited more than the clergy did, called in advance to ask permission when he rarely had to miss worship, and hugged all the children. He still drove a tractor, and had lived with his hands in God's good earth to the point that he was one with creation. I have never known a greater church member, or maybe even a more remarkable person.

"I couldn't decide what to give you, now that you're leaving," was his introductory sentence. "I bought a nice leather Bible for your family"—and coming from anybody else this would have seemed corny, but I sensed he wasn't done. He reached deep into his denim pocket, reached out his hand, the way I'd reached out mine to hand him a piece of communion bread dozens of times. Gradually he opened his crusty hand, and pressed into mine his pocket knife, worn from decades of going everywhere with him, indispensable for a country gentleman who was prepared when a string or an apple or whatever needed to be cut.

I've reflected on the profound marvel of this gift. You could have asked me, "James, list five hundred things you might vaguely hope to possess one day," and I (city slicker that I am) would never, ever have said, "Hey, a pocket knife is what I want." But here was this unspeakably invaluable treasure, pressed into my palm.

Then he added some words. "Carry that around with you in your pocket. Then some day, when you're having a bad day, feel it down in there, and remember that somebody loves you."

This shimmering, tender moment bears a little commentary. James knew how to love his preachers. In all his decades, he had loved all of us (well, there was one he said he merely "liked"), so the knife wasn't an achievement award. It was all grace, and the lovely truth that he had loved all my predecessors as well earmarked the gift more clearly to me as grace instead of something more exclusive, earned, or deserved.

Struck from Behind

The undesiredness of the knife gave me pause. I didn't want a knife, but then I didn't *not* want a knife either. How many of my sermons have been bedeviled by the notion that God satisfies our desires, that Jesus fills the yearning you have inside, and so forth. Not that God doesn't satisfy your desires, but the gift God gives is something you generally never thought of wanting, or that you had forgotten how to want. During Holy Week, the disciples weren't queueing up for crosses.

The knife was what James wanted me to have. Ever since, I have been on a seemingly futile but semi-noble campaign against gift cards and cash for Christmases and birthdays. Why are the increasingly popular cash and gift card gifts appealing? "So he can get whatever he wants" or "I don't know how to guess what she would really want"—all of which feeds into our consumer mindset that declares life is about me wanting and then getting whatever I want. Gift cards: the bane of what is really only pseudo-giving, cheap, too easy, dehumanizing giver and receiver.

God gave us what God wanted us to have. In fact, God gave us a gift that whittles away at what I stubbornly have fawned after. A knife is a sharply symbolic gift, because it cuts. How is God's Word described? "Sharper than a two-edged sword"? God's Word, which I never really asked for, prunes, severs, hacks away, like some surgical scalpel delving deeply to carve out of me what will be my undoing if it is left unattended. James gave me a knife.

And he didn't just give me a knife and say, "Here, go cut some things." As tenderly fantastic as the simple gift of the pocket knife would have been, James knew some words could be attached, should be attached, and that the words would carry the freight. "When you're having a bad day, feel it down in there, and remember that somebody loves you." We are not always sure what to make of tangible things, possessions, the stuff that comes our way. But whatever we notice out there, the shade of the tree or the grin on a face, the juiciness of an orange or the next breath I am about to take, even the crucifix hanging in the sanctuary or the sip of wine with a the taste of wafer still lingering on my palate, every good thing from God has words attached, unforgettable words we need on the bad days, memorable words for the brightest days.

Isn't that the gift I really *do* want, underneath the stuff I get duped into thinking I want? Doesn't it take a gift like James's knife to lay all this open so we finally see that God isn't so lame as to give us merely what we crave, but something infinitely richer? I think I can begin to comprehend what Hans Urs von Balthasar was learning as he prayed:

We always wanted to measure your fulfillments by the standard of our desires. More than what our hollow space contains, so we thought, we cannot obtain from you. But when your Spirit began to blow in us, we experienced so much greater space that our own standard became meaningless to us. We noticed the first installment and pledge of a wholly other freedom . . . And thus is fulfilled the promise which is the blowing Spirit itself in person: Because he blows the fulfillment toward us. He does it infallibly, if we are ready to allow ourselves to be surpassed in our desires. The religion and desire of all peoples means ultimately this: to get beyond one's own desires.[2]

A Pair of Crosses

Thinking of desire, and knives, I treasure (and frequently wear) another gift I received from another man who put on no airs and wore overalls in that upscale, dressy community—and who predeceased James (who was his friend too), although thirty years younger. Jim White was a mountain of a man, a mail carrier (like my grandfather), a devoted churchman, massive of physique, larger of spirit, one of those whose imposing body housed a humble, bowed, grateful spirit.

Jim was so big that a tumor grew to the size of a bowling ball before the doctors found it. Surgery and a battery of treatments bought him only a few months. I went to visit him and his wife Mitzi, and we talked about how to be fruitful even in one's dying days. What do we leave that says something about who we are, that those who survive can cling to and feed off the soul post-mortem?

Jim told me he liked to whittle—prompting me to share my favorite (and only) whittling joke. A city-slicker decided to venture into a rural area to see how the country folk lived. Way down a dirt road, he saw an old man in a rocking chair. He got out of his car, walked up the stony path, and asked the stranger, who was whittling, "Hey. Have you lived here all your life?" Chipping off another little slice of wood, without looking up, the man replied, "Not yet."

As soon as the words slipped out, I grimaced a little, but Jim loved the *faux pas* and laughed heartily. *Not yet* indeed. What to do with what time remains? Jim told me he had decided to do some whittling, and was fashioning little wooden crosses, with a small hole in the top, through which

2. Hans Urs von Balthasar, *The Balthasar Reader*, ed. Medard Kehl and Werner Löser; trans. Robert J. Daly and Fred Lawrence (New York: Crossroad, 1997), 431.

he would slip a little string that he then could tie to make a necklace. He'd made one for his wife, his kids, his mom, each person in his *Disciple* Bible study class, his neighbor. I felt a surge of jealousy, and hinted I might like one. He'd already made me a cross, and I wear it many Sundays, and think of Jim, his faith, and the crucifixion of Jesus on a piece of wood some men cut down and carved into a cross.

Then Jim handed me something perhaps even more spectacular. He reached under his shirt, and pulled off from around his neck another cross, not made of wood, but glittery, made of solid gold, a work of art, sheer beauty and elegance. Jim was the last person on this planet who would ever buy or own, much less wear anything fancy. I was stunned, and puzzled by the dissonance: such a simple man, such an extravagant possession. He explained that he had saved up his money for a long time, and had this cross made by a jeweler he knew. He wore it under his clothes, where no one could see—a hidden beauty, signifying to him not merely the mundane natural wood of the instrument of crucifixion, but the glory, the splendid magnificence of eternal life which was won on that cross. No one, except his wife, had ever seen it until now, and he wanted me to have it. I thought of St. Francis, and the stigmata, the mysterious wounds in his hands, feet and side he suffered late in life—but no one knew, so careful was Francis to hide the wonder of such intimacy with Christ.

The Christmas Train

But that is an explicitly religious gift, in an patently religious, pastoral context. Can we recall gifts from a long, long time ago, and notice God's presence? When I was little, my parents (like all parents, I suppose) took my

sister and me to visit Santa Claus. The funniest of all those old slides we have from the fifties shows me screaming for dear life, lunging away from Santa. No wonder: this Santa looked like he'd been ridden hard in life, not very warm and fuzzy or grandfatherly at all.

Years later, more than I will admit to now, I became the oldest child in the history of Western civilization to figure out that Santa wasn't who he said he was at all. Roaming the house one day I stumbled into my parents' closet, saw the race car I'd asked Santa to bring me—but I was such a numbskull that I scratched my head and wondered why my parents had gotten themselves such a cool toy, and whether they'd let me play with it or not. So when it appeared under the tree, and they didn't have one any longer, some synapse in my cerebrum lit up, and in one fell swoop there was no sleigh flying through the air, no elves in a North pole workshop, Santa just a dressed up guy who lived down the street. I went to my room and cried most of the afternoon. The saddest Christmas ever.

I knew little of God then. Like many people, I thought of God as a Santa Claus type figure. Old guy, white beard, lives way off somewhere, pops in mysteriously now and then bearing gifts. Surely God was "makin' a list, checkin' it twice, gonna find out who's naughty and nice . . . He knows if you've been bad or good, so be good for goodness' sake!" As a Christian minister, I've expended much effort trying to dissuade folks from imagining such a simplistic Santa Claus God—wrongly I think now. When I lost Santa, what did I have left? Just warring parents. No jolly, rotund stranger, however invisible, hatching plans to show up and bring me expressions of delight and mirth—a decent if inexact imitator of God. Maybe in my psyche, that crushing loss of Santa left a gap that God could fit into quite nicely years later.

But when Santa was still Santa, he brought me something that got raised from the dead quite unexpectedly on another Christmas decades later. As a grown person, or at least as a big person, not so grown up in spirit just yet, I was working at my home computer, hopelessly behind, the busyness of Advent and Christmas bearing down on me, stress piling up. My five-year-old son Noah insisted on playing in the room, showing me toys, grabbing at my arm, making bizarre noises.

Finally (and it is embarrassing to tell you what happened next) in exasperation I said, "Son, you just have to get out of here; Dad has so much work to do." Noah responded very calmly, but with words that crushed something in me: "Okay, Daddy, I'll leave. I don't mean to annoy you." As I turned to see him walking out, I remembered how that felt, from moments when as a little boy I'd hung my head and made sad exits.

I shut off the computer and my foolish busyness. An idea dawned on me. I pulled down those rickety attic stairs, climbed up and retrieved two grey "Red Ball" moving boxes. Inside were wads of newspaper—the

Struck from Behind

Philadelphia Inquirer, dated October 28, 1964. A huge photo of Nikita Kruschev, a box score with Johnny Unitas's stats, an ad for a Rambler. Nestled in the crumbling paper were chunks of metal track, then a caboose, an engine, a cattle car—the Lionel train set my parents gave me for Christmas in 1960, when I was five.

Midway through my connecting some of the track, Noah ambled into the room. His eyes flew wide open: "Daddy, what is this?"

"This was my train, when I was a little boy, like you—and now it's our train, together." He was duly impressed, and after a few minutes, he exclaimed, "This is the coolest toy ever. I bet this train cost a hundred dollars!" I was tempted for 1.3 seconds to calculate the value of those Lionel cars at auction—but instead I told the truth: "Oh no, son. It didn't cost a hundred dollars. It was free."

I meant *free*, as in it was a gift I simply received and didn't pay for. Then I heard the word, *free*—and who could miss the accidental yet profound analogy that at Christmas the real gift that matters, God becoming small for us in Christ, is entirely free. Like Noah walking away, we "mourn in lonely exile here until the Son of God appears." Thank God that God is not finally like Santa. No closing my eyes and hoping God might show up in the dark to meet some transient wish, like getting my work done or getting my son to chill. Thank God that God is never busy, and never annoyed. If God is our Father, God isn't the kind of busy father I'd become.

What this God gave me as a child, and gave me and Noah, costs light years more than a hundred dollars. God gives us no "thing." God gives God's own self, on the floor with children of all ages, those who are nice and those who are naughty and those who are a messy but beautiful mix of both, those who are busy and impatient, those who crave a little attention. God pokes us with a little finger, with a cry, interrupting us—thankfully. And this happens every day, and we recognize the poke in the rising of stress and weariness, or in the pressure-induced headache—a bizarre stratagem on the part of the omnipresent Christ child to bring us home to the holy, the truly memorable, the hidden plot of life unfolding according to plan.

The Worst Gift Ever

Let me return to the way the unwanted gift proves to be the best gift. I recall the precise date of the worst gift I ever received: October 22, 1965. Back then, I'd never heard of the academic term "incommensurability," the maddening reality that sometimes we talk past one another, we come at an issue with alien assumptions—and so we just miss each other. This happens in gift giving (and receiving). I wonder how many presents I have given that, for the polite receivers who never let on, were total misfires. I know I've received a few. Some become humor pieces in life: the baby blue praying hand candles I received once for performing an extremely arduous, time-consuming wedding out in the heat of August with sweat bees flying about became an object of frequent re-gifting among some of my clergy friends.

But some incommensurable gifts are harder to laugh off; unwittingly they crush the receiver. How do I recall the precise date, October 22, 1965? It was my tenth birthday, and my mother had been dropping beguiling hints for days that she had gotten me something special. I even saw the wrapped box on the dining room table—a tease to heighten the suspense. From its size I deduced that hidden inside was the one thing I wanted, needed, and simply had to have above all else: a football. Fall of the year, I was turning double digits, boys in the neighborhood were picking sides, pretending to be Johnny Unitas, Gayle Sayers, Dick Butkus. My own football: I could hardly wait.

The day came. Waiting for the little family celebration was excruciating. Cake, candles, a song . . . but none of this mattered. I wanted to grab the ball and dash down the hill to the vacant lot and meet up with Billy, David, Dwayne, Steve, break it in, toss a few touchdown passes. Proudly my mother handed me the box. I ripped through the paper, yanked open the box's top—and couldn't process what I saw. Flat, black, something shiny, what looked like a fancy pen sticking out of whatever it was. Recognizability is crucial in gift receiving; discerning that I did not know what I was looking at (and no doubt disappointed because of it) my mother announced, "I bronzed your baby shoes."

And there they were, not small white leathery things any more but as hard as the stunned shock in my heart—and with a little pen holder to boot. What to do? Melt into the floor? Sob? Scream? Turn the fountain pen into a weapon? Trained properly (and quite miraculously, I'd say in retrospect), I said what I most certainly did not feel: "Thank you."

I recalled this when I was a young preacher, and thought it illustrative of the way we sometimes think we are supposed to pray. Many of us were taught to say polite, bland, courtesy-trumping-openness prayers; and so whatever happens in life, we are to say "Thank you"—with the legendary "patience of Job" ("The Lord giveth, the Lord taketh away; blessed be the name of the Lord"). Certainly, there is some equanimity, some placid acceptance of any and all fortune and misfortune in the deeply chiseled Christian life: "I have learned, in whatever state I am, to be content. I know how to be abased, and I know how to abound; in any and all circumstances I have learned the secret of facing plenty and hunger, abundance and want" (Phil 4:11–12).

But the Bible teaches us to pray with total abandon, to shed sweet pretension and cry out; God does not mind. God welcomes the hurled, desperate prayer. We know this because downright rude prayers are enshrined in the Psalms, in Jeremiah, and even in the story of Jesus' final hours. Job himself was not patient for very long; the bulk of Job is a long-winded tirade of accusations, screams, demands, and murmuring grumbled toward the heavens.

Thinking further about the bronzed baby shoes, I wonder about a few other things now. Not only do I wonder how often I have given gifts that were not only unwanted but actually hurtful; I wonder about my words. In the course of family, friendship, work and play, how often have I tendered well-intended words that I thought would be welcomed wisdom, or craftily helpful, and have unbeknownst to me wounded someone? Or even when I've muttered something silly, off the cuff, cutting up or just filling the quiet with chatter, and have inflicted unseen hurt? What has just been overheard by someone I didn't realize was in earshot? If I knew, I'd take it all back, apologize, and make things right—but it's all past. If God was there, since I don't recall these things I've said but didn't know I was saying, then my prayer is that God somehow eased the blow, cured the hurt, and had mercy on me.

It may be that the ultimate bronzed baby shoe talk happens when we try to speak of God—especially in the face of suffering. We hope our little present of words will comfort: "She's in a better place," or "God needed another angel," or "It was God's will." But don't these little gifts of sugary comfort not only misrepresent God, but run the risk of alienating the sufferer from God by suggesting God is the enemy who ripped the beloved from your breast? Here is how James Russell Lowell responded (in poetry) to would-be comforters:

> Console if you will, I can bear it;
> 'Tis a well-meant alms of breath;
> But not all the preaching since Adam
> Has made Death other than Death.[3]

Lowell was trying to cope with the death of his daughter. Notice how the poem concludes:

> Forgive me,
> But I, who am earthly and weak,
> Would give all my incomes from dreamland
> For a touch of her hand on my cheek.
> That little shoe in the corner,
> So worn and wrinkled and brown,
> With its emptiness confutes you,
> And argues your wisdom down.

The little, unbronzed shoe lying on the floor, testimony to what was, and to what was lost. My shoes were bronzed, and will exist as such forever. But my mother who had them bronzed for me will not, and neither will I (and neither will my own children who've outgrown their shoes).

And so I ponder yet again the meaning of the shoes. I do still have those bronzed things, although I lost the pen somewhere along the way. The football I wanted so desperately, and eventually got for Christmas, is long worn out and abandoned; where do fifty-year-old footballs wind up? Fifty-year-old bronzed baby shoes wind up in my house on a shelf. Could it be that God does in fact give us what we were *not* looking for, the kind of thing that would prove bitterly disappointing to a ten-year-old but to one

3. James Russell Lowell, "After the Burial," *The Poetical Works of James Russell Lowell* (Boston: Houghton Mifflin, 1978), 309.

advancing in age makes sense? Try telling a ten-year-old whose father has died of cancer that his dad is in heaven. The crushing of spirit is harrowing; the well-meant alms of breath is instantly confuted. And yet the gift, the word that promises eternal life, is what it is. And over time, it is the only gift that matters, the one the little boy in his own old age is finally grateful for.

Hobbit Birthdays

Gifts have this surprising advent, and afterlife. James let go of the knife that was precious to him. And so I grow fonder each year of the idea of giving you, not something I went out and bought for you, but something I own, and am not especially eager to rid myself of, something that is really me—and if you have it, you'll have a piece of me. I gave Noah my most valuable Mickey Mantle cards, and I gave Sarah my most treasured, marked-up Bonhoeffer volume; Grace got my camera one year. I shared from the pulpit one time about this freakish practice, and a fourteen-year-old girl wrapped up her laptop computer (and how attached are young adolescents attached to their machines?) and gave it to her mother, whose own computer had died.

What do we give and receive? And when? And why? Birthdays: why do we receive gifts on our birthdays? J. R. R. Tolkien's smallish heroes in *The Lord of the Rings*, "hobbits," have an intriguing way of celebrating their birthdays. Instead of receiving gifts, hobbits give gifts on their birthdays. My children read about this—so as my birthday approached they suggested I give it a try. And so began our custom, stretching over several years now: on my birthday, realizing there frankly isn't anything purchasable that I want or need, I give gifts to my wife and children, never something they have bothered to ask for, just something I want them to have. They can't submit a wish list.

The best hobbit moment? Noah was seven, and due to move up to better wheels; so I got him a big bike, with red flames painted on the frame. The girls opened their hobbit gifts, and then I told him, "Let's walk out to the garage," where I had parked the new, dazzling bike right in the middle. Noah sauntered down the stairs, walked right by the thing, and looked back, wondering why we were doubled over with laughter.

Some years I've given my own stuff to others for hobbit birthday or other occasions—and as I grow older, there will be more and more of this going on. The curious virtue to giving our stuff away, instead of going to the mall to buy new stuff, is that we have less, we travel lighter, we are freer, we are not so tied down. Life, after all, is a pilgrimage; we are in exile temporarily down here—or at least so the saints of old taught us. And we find good company: when I tell friends about the hobbit birthday scheme, many of them—well, maybe just a few—decide they will see what it's like.

That's how the giving works anyhow, and may provide a clue to help us resolve issues of poverty. Jürgen Moltmann wisely suggested that "the opposite of poverty isn't property. The opposite of both poverty and property is community."[4] Then we are no longer possessed by our possessions. And our newfound poverty, even if it's only a little less affluence than what I thought I enjoyed yesterday, creates a new space, a little more room for God, and for the new friend in need God places before me.

Swept Under the Rug

Finally I think of the year I surprised Lisa with a rug for Christmas. Managing the surprise was dicey, not only because it's no small task at 2 a.m. after a day and night of Christmas Eve services to move furniture, roll up one bulky rug, lay down the new bulky rug, and replace the furniture without waking anybody up, but also because I had written a piece about the rug which *Christian Century* published earlier than expected, namely a week before Christmas.

I wasn't really planning to buy her a rug in the first place; it just showed up. Terry, from whom I had purchased a rug in Ephesus a couple of years before, reeling from the shriveled tourism in Turkey after the commencement of the war in Iraq, had brought his rugs to America and materialized in my driveway. We invited a few neighbors, who tittered with delight over Terry's wonders. Now he likes me even more, as my friends dropped thousands of dollars on rugs they weren't looking for either. Lisa looked disappointed I wasn't buying a rug I hadn't been looking for, so I sneaked Terry a check and squirreled the rug away in my neighbor's garage until Santa could retrieve it in the wee hours of Christmas morning.

But then I began to suffer theologically-induced guilt (or Scrooge-like buyer's remorse) for my compulsive purchase. Trying to hatch a sermon amid these pangs, I (insightfully, I thought) drew an analogy between a beautiful rug and my parishioners' faith. They do not disregard faith. They admire its beauty, and they are sure to get one for the living room. But then, day by day, they do not really notice the rug. They walk all over it. Should a guest pop by and ask "Oh, where did you get that rug?" they beam with

4 Jürgen Moltmann, *The Source of Life: The Holy Spirit and the Theology of Life*, trans. Margaret Kohl (Minneapolis: Fortress, 1997), 109.

pride: "From my Turkish friend Terry." Got faith? Yes, and we're proud of it. Jesus, the Turkish rug. Be sure you get one, so you can walk all over it.

Will Willimon, when he was the chaplain at Duke, was asked by a Muslim student, "Why don't the Christian students ever pray?" Five times daily, he unrolls his rug, gets down on it, and prays. The Christians?

Terry says he knows when he's going to make a sale. Eyes widen as a particular rug is unfurled; after oohing and ahhing, they get down on the floor and look at the pattern, they brush the threads, dig a finger into the pile, inquire into its history. They assume the posture of the Muslim student, but they are shopping, not praying. I got on my hands and knees, and now we own a new rug.

Terry's rug business makes me wonder. Why don't I pray so regularly? Does my ministry feel like Terry's salesmanship? Have I, as a minister, been one more peddler, teasing folks into buying that Jesus rug? Thinking more admiringly of Terry: have I thought of the people who aren't coming to buy the rugs I have to offer—and been bold enough to venture out to find them wherever they are?

We've owned the rug for some time now. I pretty much just walk over the thing. But once in a while I stop, remember Terry, and get down on my knees and study the weave, and the colors, remembering something I read a long time ago in a novel I can't locate any longer—that our lives are an alternating pattern of brightness and then dark, light hues curved against gray shadow, the overall effect being one of stunning beauty, true art that would be lost were the rug all a bright pink or cheery green. The beauty is in the pattern, the juxtaposition of it all, pain and pleasure, darkness and light, sorrow and joy. Maybe Jesus the Turkish rug wants me to get down on my knees and dig my fingers into the weave of light and dark, maybe five times each day, even if I get the rug damp with some tears.

What do I want for Christmas? Or my birthday? Or for a retirement gift? How about a little brokenness? An empty place I dare not rush to fill? How about a Jesus rug? I want to answer the Muslim student's question by using the rug, getting down on the thing, noticing its patterns, fingering the beauty of dark and light, my head bowed, letting go, finding something solid under me, holding me up, soft but not too soft, and maybe I'll take it to church so that hollow place might be a threshold even as it is lost, and found.

Chapter 11

Learning to Fly
Ruins & Gypsies

ALL MY LIFE I'VE been itching to go someplace, and after I go I'm compelled to tell about it. Travelers love to tell stories, and they must bore non-travelers to death: sagas of lost luggage, a peculiar dining experience, a flight delay, favored haunts in far-flung locales, bumping into a friend while hiking out west, the notorious flight attendant who poured coffee into my lap, the time it snowed where it never snows but we were there, etc. Nothing incites storytelling like travelling.

Why go? Paul Theroux, inimitable travel writer, could have been speaking for me when he said,

> As a child, the word "travel" did not occur to me, nor did the word "transformation," which was my unspoken but enduring wish. I wanted to find a new self in a distant place, and new things to care about. The importance of "elsewhere" was something I took on faith; "elsewhere" was the place I wanted to be. The wish to travel seems characteristically human: the desire to move, to satisfy your curiosity or ease your fears, to change the circumstances of your life, to be a stranger, to make a friend, to risk the unknown.[1]

God is in this transformation business, and it is God who has etched into our souls this restlessness, the yearning to be some place else. God loves

---

1. Paul Theroux, *The Tao of Travel: Enlightenments from Lives on the Road* (Boston: Houghton Mifflin Harcourt, 2011), ix.

curiosity, and the risk of the unknown, not to mention the vivid sense that we are on our way some place, and not entirely at home here.

My father travelled, at first to earn a living in the Air Force, and for decades afterwards as his avocation. He lost count of countries he'd visited. As a boy, I always looked forward to his homecomings. It seemed like he had missed us. His hugs were the kind that made noise, just like the ones my grandfather had doled out. And the other memorable noise was the jingle of coins, pocket change, relics of faraway countries, some I have since visited myself, some I probably will never get to, and some that don't exist any longer. A little museum of exotic coins came to be housed in an old cigar box I still possess.

Over time I've given away a bunch of foreign coins, usually when I meet the increasingly rare child who is a collector. I've picked up a few coins myself as I've travelled, sometimes because it wasn't worth exchanging them in the airport, and sometimes because I paid my own money to buy money. At Masada I bought Lisa a "widow's mite." In the secret back room of a Jerusalem antiquities dealer I purchased a Herodian piece that cost me plenty. At Ephesus I purchased a coin bearing the image of the emperor Tiberius that I hope is genuine (although I fret over being taken advantage of in such circumstances). The mite, the greenish coin with Herod's imprint, and the third bearing the likeness of Caesar, remind me that Jesus handled money. He thought God was a lot like a woman sweeping the floor looking for a tiny piece of money she really needed, and he borrowed money from the people who badgered him into saying something profound about whose image was indelibly pressed not merely into the money but within our souls.

God must not mind us travelling, and may wish for more, since most of the great heroes of the Bible and the faith were intrepid travelers, their lives with God defined largely by journeys: Abraham's pilgrimage from Ur to Hebron, Moses wandering from Egypt to Mt. Nebo, Jonah setting sail for Tarshish, Jesus setting his face toward Jerusalem, Paul trekking all over the world, St. Francis and Luther venturing to Rome, St. Ignatius and Lottie Moon traversing the globe along with a holy and unholy host of missionaries.

Yet even if we aren't explicitly on a mission for God, when we pack up and go, we see more of God's good earth. We encounter people who aren't from around here and don't look, talk, or think like we do. We can see old stones, things Jesus or the friends of Jesus might have seen and touched. We are transported out of our smallness, if only for a while. We might even become pilgrims, not merely out on the road to someplace sacred like the Camino to Santiago de Compostela or the Via Dolorosa, but also when we are walking down the sidewalk to the office or strolling the neighborhood.

Wanderlust must be strong, as the discomforts and annoyances of actual travel, delays, lost luggage, dust, the embarrassment of looking like a foolish foreigner, the lingering curse of the Tower of Babel, tensions with fellow travelers, and the odd peril of it all would otherwise keep us safely on the couch at home. Fear of flying is common, and although they tell you it's safer than the automobile, you always wonder.

Learning to Fly

My first airplane ride was nearly my last. And I forgot for nearly forty years how the story ended. Stashing me in the car, my father drove an hour or so to Wilmington, Delaware, where he had rented a small plane. He had flown everything, from B-24s to massive transports for the Air Force, and now the two of us were aloft in a little Piper Cub. Unwisely in retrospect, my dad said "Son, why don't you take the wheel?" Looked like a cinch, so as a mere third grader, I became a pilot. After a minute or so, my dad noticed we were losing a smidgeon of altitude. "Pull the wheel toward you a little so we'll climb up a bit." My pull was more of a yank than a tug—and the plane suddenly lurched into a vertical trajectory. "No, push it back down!"—and with the same gusto I mashed us into a rapid plunge. My dad seized the wheel, but the engine cut off, sputtering and then falling eerily silent. Falling indeed.

Once I was grown, I would tell this to my children, and they would always fall for the bait: "Did he get the engine started again?"—and I would tease, "No, we crashed." When my son Noah was about the age I was when I logged my first and only moments in the cockpit, my father was visiting—and the kids reminded him of this story, probably half-wondering if this were another of my tall tales. But my dad confirmed its historicity—and then told us all what I had forgotten. "We finally got back on the ground. The plane came to a stop, we climbed out—and then James took his fist and punched me in the stomach, fuming, 'You shouldn't let a little kid fly an airplane!' "

Frankly, the story was good enough before, but this added touch made it all the funnier, richer. I wonder if travel stories always bear some curious alteration in the remembering and telling. And perhaps the way we plan for, photograph, and recall a journey unveils something crucial about who we are, and what we dream of. Why, after all, on the absolute worst, most exhausting, sleeting, gale-force windy day in Paris when the kids fought and we couldn't find a place to eat, did we pose for a photo in front of the Eiffel tower—and we look like such a happy family? and why did I compound the deception by scribbling on a postcard that we were having such a great time?

On the other hand, what raucous fun was forgotten? What charmed moments immediately flew into the dusty attic of forgetfulness, never to be retrieved? How often was God there and we didn't notice, or forgot swiftly the blessing of the day? I'm thankful God can recall, and I have the suspicion that God makes heaven go on forever because that's how long we will need to review little unremembered moments when God moved, sustained, rescued, observed, chuckled, wept, and indeed was patient and merciful.

Like many boys, I suppose, I was fascinated by cars, trains, planes, rockets, all modes of transport to places like the beach, the capital, some exotic country, the moon. Even though NASA quit going to the lunar surface and thus foiled my ambition to be an astronaut, I have done all I could to fulfill that prophecy of Dr. Seuss: *Oh, the places you'll go*. I have expended far too much money traveling solo, or with friends, or hauling my family all over this globe.

Is it a restlessness? I'm sure I sported a prideful smirk when the customs guys would have to flip through seven or eight pages of visa stamps to find a blank page. I picked up a copy of Alain de Botton's *The Art of Travel*, something of a whimsical, philosophical reflection on the meaning of travel, wondering if he might offer some insights into my wanderlust. My reading began hopefully:

> If our lives are dominated by a search for happiness, then perhaps few activities reveal as much about the dynamics of this quest—in all its ardour and paradoxes—than our travels. They express, however inarticulately, an understanding of what life might be about, outside the constraints of work and the struggle for survival.[2]

But then de Botton began to explore the inevitable disappointments of travel—how the anticipation is always richer than the reality. If I am melancholy at home, I bear that with me. Travel can be exhausting, frustrating, boring—and there is inevitable disappointment.

I think that is part of why I go. Even a trip that falters beneath lofty expectations can still transform—perhaps in the same way that the ideal

2. Alain de Botton, *The Art of Travel* (New York: Vintage, 2002), 9.

of love is never fully experienced, but yet we still love, even if awkwardly. I think of pilgrims in ancient times: great caravans made their way to Jerusalem for the high holy days of Passover or Shavuot, and guilt-ridden medieval people left everything behind to snake their way to Chartres or the Holy Sepulchre. Martin Luther ventured to Rome, and was not edified but appalled. The shock of a strange encounter, the curtains flung open in a faraway place expose the truth about life back home more than we realize.

A Gypsy near London

As our train ambled beyond the outskirts of London, I thought I would kill some time by quizzing my children on a few items I'd tried to instill in their brains: "How did the Gettysburg address begin?" "Who comprised the Second Triumvirate?" "Can you count to ten in Spanish?"

When I asked, "Can you name the books of the Bible?" another train-rider across the aisle turned, and his eyes zoomed in on us. I had noticed him earlier, sitting with a little boy; he seemed to want to chat with me, but I averted my gaze, not at all eager to meet anybody on the last day of vacation. I was soon to find out that he was a gypsy. He watched expectantly as my son began, "Genesis, Exodus . . ." and when there was an extended hesitation just before "1 Chronicles," the man interrupted the recitation (to my children's relief). Excitedly, in a charming cockney accent, he asked, "Are you a Christian, man?"

His question felt different from the annoyingly pious peddler of pamphlets you bump into in America, inquiring sanctimoniously, "Are you saved?" I replied in the affirmative, which led him to ask, "What *kind* of a Christian are you?" Such a good question. How to answer? A not as devoted as I wish to be kind of Christian? A cynical on Mondays Christian? Orthodox yet progressive? I kept it simple: "Methodist."

"Methodist?" He shook his head, as if I had just told him I suffer from some chronic disease. "Where *I* come from, Methodists don't take their faith seriously, they just go through the motions, it has no real impact on their lives, it's just a social thing." I assured him, "Oh, we don't have that problem where *I* come from." My oldest child barely restrained a fairly audible groan.

Then he launched into a lengthy description of the gypsy church, how even though other churches across Europe barely register a pulse, the gypsy church is booming, growing, vital, even if unnoticed. In Hungary, Spain, France, Italy, and England, gypsies are being converted, and are joining thriving bodies of believers. As my new friend—Caleb Jones was his name—explained, it isn't easy for gypsies to become disciples of Jesus. "Do you know what the most common, and best paid profession is for gypsies?" I harbored a guess or two in my mind but didn't reply. "Fortune-teller. And when you become a Christian, you can't be a fortune-teller any more. So people have to give up their livelihood, and support of their families. We're asking a lot."

I explored this with him, asking if they couldn't just pretend, since fortune-telling isn't real anyhow. But no, fortune-telling dabbles in the occult, and claims for itself what is not true, so the new Christian who would be serious about his or her faith must immediately desist from fortune-telling. An extended pause in our conversation ensued—during which I pondered what professions American Christians would never forsake, all the careers of fortune-making upon which the church ventures no meaningful opinion, fortune-making which dabbles in much that is not true, and is not of God. The gypsy church is "asking a lot," and it is booming. In America, we ask for next to nothing.

I noticed Caleb's young son was holding a book with the alphabet, and some simplistic, basic reading sentences. Naively I thought this lad was learning to read. But it was Caleb's book. "Gypsies don't go to school, and gypsies don't read. But I am training to be a minister—like you!—and so I have to learn to read. It's hard . . . but I can't wait until I can read God's Word—like you!" In my mind, I rifled through the many books in my bag I'd brought to read on our junket, novels, biographies, tour books . . . and at about that moment the train screeched to a halt at the station. Our families gathered up the bags, and then lingered on the station platform to say goodbye. My gypsy friend had one last question. "What are you doing tonight? We have a service at half-seven, lots of gypsies coming. We would love for you to come." I looked at my wife and remembered our family's grand plan to grab a bite and then watch the movie, *Scooby-do*.

I think in that moment I perceived all that was wrong with the church, and in me. Simultaneously I had just met the hope of the church, in a gypsy, who like the Son of Man had no place to lay his head. His name, after all, was Caleb, namesake of Joshua's friend who scouted out enemy territory and believed God would deliver. This Caleb lured us away from the movie house into a raucous service of humble prayer and holy praise with some ex-fortune-tellers, with his lingering, perfectly targeted question, "What kind of a Christian are you?"

Old Rocks

What kind of a traveller are you? A trope my children seem to parrot quite routinely goes something like this: "Vacations? Dad never took us to Disneyworld. He only took us to see old rocks." I'm not much interested in places that don't have old rocks. Even the newer places: Normandy is a marvel for those of us obsessed by World War II, but there are also stunning medieval cathedrals, and even old Roman ruins. The Louvre has plenty of art only a couple of centuries old, but I find myself drawn to the original medieval fortress underground. In London most people want to see Buckingham Palace or Big Ben, but I want to delve underground to things more ancient, or actually to get out of the city into the countryside where I can find the ruins of Hadrian's Wall.

I wonder if my children even remember some of our adventures: trying out the acoustics at the theater of Epidaurus, a competitive foot race at Delphi, sticking a hand in the mouth of truth at Santa Maria in Cosmedin

in Rome (just like Audrey Hepburn and Gregory Peck in *Roman Holiday*), strolling the streets of Corinth. One whole vacation was a castle tour of Wales, where Llewellyn ab Iorwerth lived and fought in places like Criccieth and Dolwyddelyn. Another was a cathedral tour of France, St. Denis being our favorite, history's first church with an ambulatory *and* clerestory windows, with all those tombs dating back to Clovis and Childebert in the sixth century. A massive wooden door of York Minster ripped a nail off Sarah's big toe, and snow fluttered down through the oculus when we gazed upward in the Pantheon.

Talk about old: on our wild west tour we climbed up into thousand-year-old dwellings at Mesa Verde—but those are newbies compared to the simple age of the terrain itself at Canyon deChelles. American places are special, although my kids sometimes sneered: Oh, this is *only* two hundred years old? Noah and I studied the wall and sunken road at Fredericksburg, Boston's cemetery featuring Sam Adams, Crispus Attucks, and Mother Goose herself, and quite a few forts, my personal favorite being Fort Pulaski, built by Robert E. Lee outside Savannah. Such an important spot for me: I have in the forest of many darker childhood memories a few clearings of light, laughter and love, and they seem to have happened here. We have slides of me as a little boy with my parents and sister picnicking on these grounds, climbing the walls, imagining the Civil War battle, and the lingering peace. Not surprisingly, I drove my own wife and children back there decades later—but why? Just to see the place? To try to recapture a happy memory? Or to heal what was broken?

Why this obsession with old ruins? Archaeology is a fascinating endeavor anybody could dig (pun intended), and the ancient world holds me in thrall for reasons I will never comprehend. I don't think it's a "past lives" type of thing, although if I could choose a past life it might be in ancient Rome or medieval Paris. I read a quirky novel about a man who had hauled his family all over the place to visit the remains of buildings and walls from antiquity. Guilty over the mess of his marriage, he laments, "I have ruined her life again, a lifelong passion for ruins thrown back in my face."[3] Could that be it—a ruined life, dragging others into ruin? I shudder, and then think better of myself and these noble junkets.

Some deep wisdom must linger upon or even within those old rocks. If a stone somebody hewed a couple of thousand years ago has stuck around, I want to look, gawk, maybe touch, and wonder. After all, Jesus saw some of those ruins. Some of the stones were chiseled and put in place by St. Francis. There is an old stone baptismal font not far from where I live. When the Benedictines built their cathedral at Belmont Abbey, they reworked a stone that had been used as a trading block for slave auctions; the transformation of the offending stone into one giving life is proclaimed in the plaque attached to the font: "Upon this rock, men once were sold into slavery. Now upon this rock, through the waters of Baptism, men become free children of God."

3. Tod Wodicka, *All Shall Be Well; And All Shall Be Well; And All Manner of Things Shall Be Well* (New York: Vintage, 2007), 73.

How much affection does God have for that stone? God made the thing a few billion years back, it lay around for a few millennia, then was put to perverse use that angered God. But then to God's giddy delight that old stone found its way into a church, held water for the thing Jesus told us to do to people, and now speaks to us. Each one of us, after all, is (as Marilynne Robinson suggested) "a little civilization built on the ruins of any number of preceding civilizations"—and what better might we have to bequeath to those who survive us than "the ruins of old courage, and the lore of old gallantry and hope"?[4]

Christopher Lasch was right: "Children need to learn about faraway places and olden times before they can make sense of their immediate surroundings."[5] When we go places, as children or as adults, we get jolted out of our complacency, and discover a need for courage and hope. One afternoon, our family was walking back to the hotel from the catacombs in Rome, and we noticed graffiti all over the sidewalks denouncing our American President, George Bush. Then a woman, standing in a door, accosted us. "Are you Americans? Come in, come in, I have to show you something." Her urgency wasn't to be denied, so we entered the building.

She led us to a television where we saw a huge crowd of Italians weeping. A funeral? And then between the TV images and the woman's gesturing and broken English, I realized it was the burial of an Italian journalist, a young woman, brutally killed in Baghdad trying to report on the Gulf War. Her repeated litany: "You get Bush, we get this." Just as Christians in the earliest centuries got caught in the crossfire of Roman imperial policy, we felt quite keenly in this faraway place how enmeshed we all are in history's unfolding in the daily news, and how it all seems from the very different perspective of a modern Roman.

So Lisa and I have taken our children all over the world, and each junket (to the Cotswolds, Wales, Rome, Paris, Greece, Normandy) could supply grand and funny tales. But now we turn instead to another kind of travel, not simply the kind when you view old rocks, but the sort of trip you take in order perhaps even to become holy. Some might say we go on mission trips to do good, but I've never accomplished much that's solid enough to show for my efforts. I have, however, met some of God's closest friends, and been haunted and changed bit by bit because of these encounters.

4. Marilynne Robinson, *Gilead* (New York: Farrar, Straus, and Giroux, 2004), 197, 246.

5. Christopher Lasch, *The Revolt of the Elites and the Betrayal of Democracy* (New York: Norton, 1995), 159.

Chapter 12

Saints Abroad
Holy People, Holy Places

IN 1985 I SIGNED on to go to Fuzhou, a mid-sized city by China's standards, with my ethics professor at Duke, Creighton Lacy. He had lived there as a boy until his family was exiled by Mao's regime in 1948—all except his father, who had been the Methodist bishop of Fuzhou. Last the family had heard, Bishop Lacy was in prison; for thirty-seven years they had received no news of his fate.

One night while we were there, a man, someone Dr. Lacy recalled from childhood, came by the hotel and told us his story. He had been imprisoned with Bishop Lacy, who was treated cruelly and became deathly ill; no doctor was called to the jail. Finally, he died there, in his friend's arms. The night after we learned the awful truth, we worshipped together. I watched Dr. Lacy, with his friend, in front of a mixed body of American and Chinese Christians, reading words from another prisoner, Paul, which will always ring differently for me:

> If God is for us, who is against us?. . . Who shall bring any charge against God's elect? Who shall separate us from the love of Christ? Shall tribulation, or distress, or persecution, or famine, or nakedness, or peril, or sword? As it is written, "For thy sake we are being killed all the day long; we are regarded as sheep to be slaughtered." No, in all these things we are more than conquerors through him who loved us. For I am sure that neither death, nor life, nor angels, nor principalities, nor things present, nor things to come, nor powers, nor height, nor depth,

nor anything else in all creation, will be able to separate us from
the love of God in Christ Jesus our Lord (Rom 8:31–39).

Travelling Light

When she was a teenager, Sarah went with me to visit a Methodist congregation in Siauliai, Lithuania, a smallish church just coming out from under the thumb of the Soviets. Their sanctuary was barely a hut; they were
quite proud of their newly installed bathroom with running water. Sunday
came, and I read from Philippians—in sketchy Lithuanian I'd practiced.
My pronunciation had to be laughable, but the people of God could not
stifle their tears as they heard Paul's words:

> Paul and Timothy, servants of Christ Jesus, to all the saints
> at Philippi: grace to you and peace from God our Father and
> the Lord Jesus Christ. I thank my God in all my remembrance
> of you, always in every prayer of mine for you all making my
> prayer with joy, thankful for your partnership in the gospel from
> the first day until now. And I am sure that he who began a good
> work in you will bring it to completion at the day of Jesus Christ.
> It is right for me to feel thus about you all, because I hold you
> in my heart, for you are all partakers with me of grace, both in
> my imprisonment and in the defense and confirmation of the
> gospel (Phil 1:1–7).

That afternoon we were driven to Lithuania's holiest shrine, the "hill of
crosses," an unforgettable, sacred place: decades ago, beleaguered Christians erected a few crosses, which the Soviets tore down, only to be replaced during the night by more crosses, then more and more, until
today there are literally hundreds of thousands of crosses jammed onto a
single mound. To our surprise, we discovered an adjacent monastery with
stained glass devoted to the life of St. Francis, including his naïve, bold
enactment of Jesus' words, "Sell all you have a give to the poor," returning
the very clothes off his back to his chagrined father.

So, it was in the company of Christians who'd struggled much, and of
St. Francis, that I learned the value of luggage. The day came to fly home
from Lithuania. I was packing—and feeling a bit grumpy, weary after
weeks of travel, anticipating the drudgery of long waits, checking and then
probably losing bags, the line through customs getting bogged down, my
herniated disk inflamed. Perhaps St. Francis whispered something to me
about the way he parted with his clothing—for out of the blue I had this

thought: Why don't I just leave my clothes and the big suitcase here? I'll sail right through customs, my back won't ache from hauling the luggage.

So I started to unpack. Pants, another pair of pants, a shirt, a tie, a jacket, another shirt. This was getting to be fun, thinking of the young men I'd met who would feel cooler in these American clothes than I'd ever felt in them. But then there was a sweater—the sweater my wife had just given me for Christmas, beautiful, carefully chosen. Okay, I'll leave most of my clothes, but take this sweater home.

But then what would Lisa think? Hadn't I married the kind of woman who would be annoyed with me if I left most of my clothes, but thought her sweater was too good to leave behind? So I left that one too. And I can tell you that I have enjoyed all of those clothes, and especially the new Christmas sweater, far more knowing they are being worn by friends in Lithuania than if I had them in my wardrobe at home. I haven't gone naked one day since then. And I was afforded a small taste of what Francis understood so well, and the rich young ruler did not: the joy of giving it all away.

Regina the Banshee

Eager as I am now to speak of my several visits to the places St. Francis knew and loved, I'm constrained to linger in Lithuania for one more story. Five years after leaving my clothes in Siauliai, my daughter Grace and I were part of a building team in Birzai, where we were renovating an old Soviet recruiting station—although "recruiting" would be a sunny euphemism for what really happened there. Lithuanians were "enlisted," or actually stiff-armed, into service to the Soviet military machine. What delicious irony: a building where those who were not free were compelled to serve a nefarious regime being spruced up to function as a place where hymns, scripture, prayers and sermons would set people free.

Grace and I learned we would be staying in the home of someone named Regina, whom we quickly discovered to be gregarious, hospitable but not fussy, more eager to talk about God than the weather. You and I might think of Regina as poor. Our small, cramped quarters did not feature running water—although it took us two days to realize the toilet didn't actually flush. Regina's husband, who'd lost a leg due to inadequate health care years before, hobbled down to the creek while we slept to fill buckets with water to pour into the tank so we soft Americans wouldn't feel inconvenienced.

Regina was obviously a woman of immense faith. Like so many people in eastern Europe, she had grown up as an atheist. After she'd raised
her children, she got to know the handful of women that were the heart of
the fledgling Methodist congregation in Birzai, began to study the Bible,
and then became a sledgehammer of belief and action. She had bragged
to me about a little ministry she and the women ran: these women we'd
rank as poor spent three days each week giving what little they had to the
women *they* regarded as poor, those who lived in the "villages," remote,
outlying areas of extreme poverty. "Would you like to see our work?" she
asked. It doesn't take much for me to abandon manual labor, even if it is
mission-related, so I said yes.

We stopped by the grocery store, and I gleefully filled basket after
basket with essentials, and paid for it all with somebody else's money,
plunking down the church credit card. I had no authorization or budget,
so I made an on-the-spot, Robin Hood-like decision to steal from the rich
to give to the poor. Then we drove out of the city.

That's correct: *we* drove. At first, Regina drove—like a banshee. She
mashed the gas pedal as hard as she could, bounding over curbs and then
skimming the edges of ditches, crushing bushes that frankly weren't on the
road, backed into a tree, jostling the food in the back out of the bags—as if
she wanted to get to her destination right now, not in an hour; she pressed
that ramshackle old rusty car to keep pace with her missionary zeal. After
we got out and pushed the car out of some mud she'd driven into, she
asked me in exasperation, "Will you drive?" *Good Lord, yes I'll drive.*

The first woman we visited lived in a tiny clapboard house—"house"
being used loosely for this cold, breezy, varmint-infested awful excuse for
shelter where she was raising her four children. As we approached, Regina
told me she was gravely concerned about this woman's romantic situation:
seems she had fallen in with a man Regina suspected of drinking, and being lazy. Regina banged her fist on what passed as a door, and we made our
way in. The mom, I thought, would have been some sort of beauty where I
lived, married to a doctor or lawyer and putting her kids in private school.
But here she was poor, and embarrassingly so even by Lithuanian standards. She blushed, smiled and said "Thank you" (and jabbed her children
with her elbows to remind them to say the same) as we placed what were
thankfully non-perishables on a wobbly table as a few roaches scattered.

Then Regina got close to the woman, looming over her, wagging a
finger in her face, and spoke sternly for quite a long time—a lecture about
the ne'er-do-well boyfriend, no doubt. The woman cowered, but bore it as

best she could. Rising to a crescendo of vehemence, Regina wound up her tirade, then paused, held out her arms to us and the children, and sweetly said, "Now let us pray." And she prayed—at length, in Lithuanian, then in English, displaying a shimmering intimacy and strong urgency with God who most certainly hears such prayers. She thanked God for us, prayed about various health or learning challenges the children were facing, and then called down a curse on the soon-to-be ex-boyfriend. That poor guy was in some trouble.

In all my days, I have never seen such stellar mission work. Regina, with virtually no resources except the little bit she and her handicapped husband could muster (but also with her extraordinary determination), banded together with other women like her, and went out to their poor. They didn't simply drop off the goods; they got involved in their lives. Fearlessly she castigated her poor friend about a relationship she knew would harm her; and she prayed, offering blunt pleas to God on her behalf. And then we went to more such homes, until the food ran out.

Grace filmed an interview I conducted with Regina in which she spoke of coming to faith in Christ, her love for her little church, and her ministry in the villages. I asked her, "Why do you do this?"—and she frowned, puzzled I would ask such a silly thing. "This is just what Christians do, isn't it?" When we left for the airport the next day, I simply asked her to pray for us, and I am sure she has, and does and will, and I take comfort in being prayed for by someone who knows how to do what I could never in a million years figure out how to do: deliver food, a lecture, and a prayer.

And I will forever fight anybody who says *Don't send money overseas; we have problems right in our own backyard*, or to anybody who says *Don't just send money anywhere; that reinforces dependency.* In our back yard we don't know how to lecture anybody; we only fume in the smug privacy of our own heads over somebody we don't know. And dependency? I find myself strangely dependent upon Regina, and cannot think of many better uses of money I happen to have than to send it to her. She depends on it.

Suburb of Heaven

Perhaps I recognized this modern day, real life St. Francis in a former Soviet bloc country because of an earlier travel encounter I'd had with St. Francis himself. In October of 1984 I found myself in Rome visiting a friend, a Catholic priest who was studying theology in Italy. To me, making such a journey, and knowing a priest there personally, felt a little chic. Phillip suggested we take the train to Assisi. Little did I know I would return there many times, not as a sightseer but as a pilgrim, dragging others along so they might feel what I felt there.

Phillip and I stepped off the train, and there it was, to the east, the medieval, terraced, walled city where Francis had grown up, beckoning us to come. Standing in the same spot, Pope John XXIII described it eloquently:

> Assisi is surely a suburb of heaven. Here we are truly at the gates
> of paradise. Why did God give Assisi this aura of sanctity, almost
> suspended in the air, which the pilgrim feels almost tangibly? So
> that men will recognize their creator and recognize each other
> as brothers.[1]

A taxi hauled us and our things to a lovely pensione, our base for three days of walking, sitting in churches, kneeling in prayer, conversing. I picked up a copy of *The Little Flowers of St. Francis* and read its quaint stories of the saint's life.

At night, despite the comforts of the pensione, I simply could not sleep. I would drift off easily, but then I would waken at 1:00 or 2:00 a.m. Although I do not have a mystical bone in my body, and generally chuckle in disdain when I hear of spiritual encounters, I feel fairly certain that Francis himself was shaking me out of my slumber each night, refusing

1. Arnaldo Fortini, *Francis of Assisi*, trans. Helen Moak (New York: Crossroad, 1981), 86.

to let me sleep. When he lived in Assisi, he did not sleep much, and his friends reported that he frequently prayed all night long. Was he lurking in my room?

I do not know. I have returned to Assisi a number of times, and have read a decent percentage of what has been published about St. Francis. I've written about him myself, and he pops up in sermons and conversations. Franciscan images hang on the walls of my office and home: Cimabue's serene fresco with the unforgettably gentle face of Francis, the Romanesque crucifix which miraculously spoke to Francis, posters of the Giotto frescoes capturing dramatic moments in his life.

Funny thing about icons. For a long time I thought of them as mnemonic devices to call to mind my role models: I see Francis, so I try to be a little bit more like Francis. But now the icons feel different to me: I see Francis, yet it seems he is looking back at me. An icon is like a window between heaven and our world, through which the saints—Francis, or my grandparents, or a holy host of others represented pictorially in my various spaces—are watching me, observing my life, raising an eyebrow now and then, asking a few questions, cheering me on. At times I am embarrassed and think seriously about draping a towel over Francis's face, or Jesus's. But then I let the conversation happen. And it is good, helpful, and I find myself drawn a little bit closer to the Jesus Francis knew so intimately.

My return trips to Assisi have all been provocative, each journey in its own peculiar way. In 2007, I led a group of teenagers to Assisi—most of them having grown up as privileged as Francis himself. I watched them carefully to see what would happen. Would they feel the presence of Francis? Would the young women recognize Francis's younger friend Clare? Would this be mere sightseeing, or something richer, a defining moment in their lives? Might one or two throw away all or even fragments of the privileged life they could easily enjoy and gravitate toward sainthood?

Day by day we walked where Francis walked, and made arduous climbs. We found rocks, caves, masonry joined to natural stone, modestly marked in Italian or occasionally English with signs basically declaring "Francis slept here," or "Francis prayed here." Old rocks.

We hiked four kilometers up to the Eremo delle Carceri, the beautiful hermitage looming above Assisi where Francis prayed. We traipsed around the Rieti valley and saw a small red cross Francis painted inside a stone chapel, and the spectacular sanctuary at Greccio where the saint orchestrated history's first live nativity. We even ventured far north to LaVerna where Francis was literally wounded by God with the stigmata, mysterious gashes in his hands, feet, and side which I believe were not self-inflicted but mystical gifts from Jesus whom Francis wanted so desperately to imitate. In the evenings after dinner we delved more deeply into what we had seen together, and then we held hands and prayed.

I had given each teenager a little gift months before: a wooden image of Francis with the prayer he prayed over and over, day by day, when he was restless, troubled, trying to divine what God wanted of him. I knew we would visit San Damiano where he prayed these words, and could view the very crucifix before which he prayed. So they were prepared when we finally knelt there, bowed our heads, then gazed up at the face of Jesus, and uttered very old words, reliable words, a prayer for a lifetime:

> Most high, glorious God,
> enlighten the darkness of my heart
> and give me, Lord,
> correct faith,
> firm hope,
> perfect charity,
> wisdom and perception,
> that I may do
> what is truly your most holy will.

After praying this prayer over and over in front of this Jesus, Francis heard Jesus say something from the cross: "Rebuild my church, for as you can see it is falling into ruin." I found myself wishing Jesus would speak, half believing he might at any moment. I worried that perhaps he just did, but I was tone-deaf and missed it. I keep little cards with this prayer in my top desk drawer at the office, in my sock drawer at home, and in the little junk compartment that sits under my right elbow when I drive. I wonder if those teenagers, now grown, remember, or if they've kept the wooden impress of his prayer—and if they ever pray to know and do God's most holy will.

Pilgrimages to the Holy Land

But my most beloved place, if I were pressed to choose, would have to be Israel, the Holy Land, Palestine. What do we call this place? I have been many times, leading groups, or on my own. Once I got to spend a week in and around Jerusalem with archaeologists Shimon Gibson and James Tabor. I took a group during the Intifada when tourists just weren't taking the risk of being in the Holy Land, and we enjoyed the absence of crowds, singing Christmas carols in the Basilica which marks the place of Jesus's birth. I have witnessed ugliness between Israelis and Palestinians. I've climbed the snake path of Masada a few times, and battled crowds, heat, and the endless press of souvenir hawkers. I snapped a photo as Sarah, aged eight, got bitten by a camel.

Every time I return from Israel, I'm a bit startled by well-meaning friends who breathe a sigh of relief, tell me they have prayed intently for my safety, and yet look a bit puzzled why any rational person would venture into such a place. There are plenty of perils for the pilgrim to Israel: an injection of uneasiness about our vapid culture here, a keen sense that Jesus was real and my faith had better be real also, and the omnipresent possibility of a sprained ankle from walking around on loose stoned pavements that are seven times as old as the United States. But I've never thought the Iranians or Syrians would target my little bus of American tourists. To me, Israel feels safer than back home.

Mark Twain ventured to Israel, and penned a host of wry musings (in *Innocents Abroad*) about his experience in Palestine; and I can only say *Amen* to his shrewd thought that "travel is fatal to prejudice, bigotry and narrow-mindedness, and many of our people need it sorely on those accounts. Broad, wholesome, charitable views of men and things cannot be acquired by vegetating in one little corner of the earth all one's lifetime."[2]

What is so special about this little corner of the planet called Israel? We know its historical importance, squatting at the crossroads of civilizations and the three big religions. And if you're into Jesus or more generally the Bible, to see the place is an enormous privilege. I think for me, the virtue of being with other people in Israel is some sort of telescoped embodiment of what we do (or should be doing) every Sunday: sitting in pews, we hear scripture read out loud, and try to envision the Jordan river, the stones of the temple, the lapping waves of Galilee. The pilgrim in Israel realizes the images are not merely spiritual but rather quite earthy and tangible. Archaeologists discovered a fishing boat from the first century, and when you study its stunningly preserved wooden beams, you realize this is a boat that Jesus saw, and perhaps stepped into for a few hours or even days.

It's a small place. The Jordan doesn't quite qualify as a "river"; "winding creek" might be more descriptive. Capernaum is a teeny-tiny place. Mark 2 tells us Jesus left the synagogue and went home; that very house, which archaeologists discovered, is no more than twenty steps away.

2. Mark Twain, *The Innocents Abroad* (New York: Modern Library, 2003), 491.

Nazareth is a bit of a boomtown now, but in Jesus' day the population might have been forty or a hundred. Galilee is merely a small lake. You can drive the length and breadth of the country in no time flat. Mount Tabor is a little hill by our standards.

I like the smallness, not for the convenience of touring, but in consideration of the nature of the gospel. God became small—and life is about small things. Would we really prefer a God who came down in a metropolis and then ventured at supersonic speed all over the globe? Not me. What matters in my world is small: my children in their cribs, a little note my wife leaves me, a hug, a smile, words of affection, a short walk to the mailbox to open a birthday card, that breath I just took, and the unexpected rapidity of the passing of a lifetime that makes you gasp. We know God in the smallness of our mundane existence, in the seeming irrelevance of a single life played out by a little lake ringed by a few hills.

Think of all the history and grandeur wedged into such a small tract of land: a stone age tower in Jericho predating Joshua by eight thousand years, a wall David built to defend his palace, a tunnel Hezekiah hewed out of rock to retrieve water during the Assyrian invasion, a house burnt by Nebuchadnezzar, a box that once held the bones of the high priest Caiaphas, massive stones from Herod's buildings (including his winter getaway at Masada), the stunning Dome of the Rock (Islam's historic shrine), Crusader dungeons in Acco. Once I saw a double rainbow in the valley below Nazareth! But beneath that rainbow, jarringly out of place, were the golden arches of McDonald's. More hauntingly, the landscape is littered with barbed wire, war's debris, and armed citizens, their faces hardened by years, even centuries, of tension. The ironies, the wonders, the stress, the sorrow: God chose such a place to reconcile the world to God's own self. How could it be otherwise?

Everything that happened in the Bible is marked by a church or a tacky memorial. You can see Lot's wife, or Adam's tomb, or the inn of the Good Samaritan. There aren't one or two but actually three places that claim to be the real Emmaus. Even archaeologists "find" bogus things—like the much ballyhooed burial box of James the brother of Jesus, which proved to be a not-so-clever forgery. Fred Craddock tells of being on a tour that visited the Upper Room. The group just ahead of his was led by a pastor who told his flock, with gripping emotion, "This is the very room where Jesus shared the last supper with his disciples. You are sitting on the very seats where they sat . . ." And then they had communion, prayed, and left. Craddock's group then entered, and the tour guide pointed to the walls and arched ceiling and explained "Now we can tell that this is a sixteenth- or seventeenth-century building, the real last supper plainly not having taken place anywhere in this vicinity." A woman next to Craddock whispered to him, "I wish I were in that other group."

But I never want to be in that other group. I want the real thing. So when I go to the recently excavated Pool of Siloam, I can sit on the very stones where Jesus stood, taught, and healed. On the southern edge of the Temple Mount I can stand on the very steps Jesus would have used when teaching and entering the temple. His feet and my feet pressed on the same stones—separated by two millennia, yes, but still as close as one can dream of getting. I want to go barefooted, or press my face into the stones—but why? In my heart, and in my daily routine, I somewhat vaguely want to be close to Jesus; but I really do want to get closer, and maybe walking where he quite literally walked will, if only for a few moments, get me in touch with him as I might see and feel what he experienced.

I saw a woman praying at the Wailing Wall—not at the outdoor plaza, but down the tunnel, in the dark, at the very point we think is closest to the ancient Holy of Holies. I know Israelis don't call it the Wailing Wall any more, but the "Western" Wall—but this woman was wailing. Her Bible was open, and pressed with her right hand against her face, getting soaked with her tears; her body was bobbing, oscillating, her vocal sobbing was harrowing to hear, and see. I wanted to tap her on the shoulder and find out what passage her Bible was open to, against her grieving visage—and what was her story? Or I wanted to comfort her—or better, to see if her heart might be transplanted into my chest so I could pray as she was praying. I do not see this at home.

If I had to summarize the churches, altars, and art in Israel, words like "garish," "tacky," "kitsch," and "gaudy" come to mind—but I find myself not minding. I admire the piling on of devotion. Nobody waited for fine Renaissance artists or elegant decorators to build around holy places. Whoever was devoted threw up what they knew and could muster. Some pilgrims are put off by the crowds: you poke your way into the most sacred of all sites, the Church of the Holy Sepulchre, and it's just a mob; you will get shoved. But what if those buildings sat empty? I like it that Koreans and Germans and Hispanics all save up their hard-won money to go to this place, when there are so many beaches and resorts and Las Vegases that beckon.

Yes, part of the ugliness of the most sacred nation, and the most holy places in that nation, is that turf wars threaten to spoil it all. Because of

Jerusalem, the world can't seem to be at peace; the roof of the Church of the Holy Sepulchre will probably cave in before the Catholics, Copts, Greeks, and Armenians can agree on repairing it. But even this elicits my affection: I like it when a place or an idea is contested, even fiercely. Something matters—in a world where nothing much seems to matter, unless you count what movie stars wore to the Oscars or who's still standing in a reality show.

In Israel, I feel small, and thus empowered. More than any place on earth, Israel forces me to realize what has been done for me. It's like the beach: for me, if I'm in the mountains or even another country, I scribble a list of things to do to keep busy and get it all in; but at the beach I can just sit, and stare, for hours. In Israel, I do move around busily; but I sit, and stare, and don't feel I'm the master of my own existence. In this place, God did things, amazing things that resonate through the centuries. God acted here, for me, and for the group some of us heard sing "How Great Thou Art" in Korean, for everybody back home, and even for those who don't believe, or don't know the story.

The stones tell the story of the centuries. Archaeological sites (like the pool of Bethesda, where Jesus healed) feel messy, with modern walkways perched on Crusader walls that reused Byzantine stones which in turn obscure Herodian foundations. But instead of feeling confused, I feel it's all right there, past and present, all pasts and all presents, embraced in a single web of rock and wonder. I am part of something bigger than myself, something older, something that transcends me and my little world. I find myself invited into the adventure of the ages, one that will culminate at the end of time in nothing else but a rousing chorus of praise to the God who made it all and loved it all so patiently.

For you see, a pilgrimage to the Holy Land symbolizes what life is really all about, and also our final destination. "I am bound for the promised land" was a hymn my grandparents sang. They never got out of the Carolinas much, and never were afforded the nearly elitist privilege of travelling all the way to Jerusalem. But they knew the Jesus who stood on the stones, and vested their lives and fortunes in the journey to God's new Jerusalem.

Chapter 13

Another Day Blown
My Life with Books

SOMETIMES, I FEEL A little embarrassed at how much money I have spent on books, how much in those books I can't recall any longer, how much time I might have spent bowling or learning to jitterbug or simply sleeping. I could have purchased a Bentley, or mastered woodworking, or Italian cooking, or maybe golf with the staggering amount of time I have spent with my head in some book. Maybe I should have prayed more. What will happen to all these books when I die?

I like to imagine that after I have died, I will enjoy what I hope will be heaven's peculiar privilege: to converse with my favorite authors, or even their subjects, real and fictional. That might take a while though, as it's quite a crowd, a holy and unholy fellowship without whom I might be more holy, but probably less so. I'm sure I'd be bored without them, and more lonely.

My particular experience of reading isn't special (except to me, of course), although it does occur to me that without the throng of books that choke my extensive shelving, I would not know God nearly so well, or myself, or others. And the books that help me know are not all theological or even PG. A crass novel, an atheistic manifesto, and the biography of an evil megalomaniac can all be used by God—which leads me to my personal favorite among many quotations about the place of books, penned by Thomas Merton:

> Reading ought to be an act of homage to the God of all truth. We
> open our hearts to words that reflect the reality He has created

or the greater Reality which He is. It is also an act of humility and reverence towards other men who are the instruments by which God communicated His truth to us. Reading gives God more glory when we get more out of it, when it is a more deeply vital act not only of our intelligence but of our whole personality, absorbed and refreshed . . . Books can speak to us like God, like men or like the noise of the city we live in.[1]

I was not reared to be a reader. My mother owned a few little pastel devotional guides. A couple of leather-bound Bibles lay on the coffee table in our home. I do not recall even once seeing either of my parents sitting in a chair or in the bed reading any book. As a child, I did not care for books, although in elementary school I tested fairly well as a reader. Reading assignments, even through high school, made me bristle, and I rifled through *Cliff's Notes* after running up the white flag of boredom twenty pages in to *Moby Dick* or *The Great Gatsby* or *The Secret Sharer*.

Blowing a Whole Day

Yet by fits and starts, little intimations began to suggest the wonder reading would become. Somehow, when I was in fifth or sixth grade, I held in my hands a copy of Jack London's *The Call of the Wild*. I do not know why, but I sat on the wooden stairs that descended into our unfinished cement block basement, and started to read. I did not move from that step until I had turned the last page. How many hours had flown by? Did anybody miss me? I didn't miss myself. By some miracle of space-time transport I had found myself in snowy northlands, and my absorption in the dog-sledding venture was total. Maybe a year or two later—and I think this was a school assignment—I read Jesse Stuart's *The Thread that Runs So True* in maybe two sittings. When I put the book down, I swore I was going to become a teacher in rural Appalachia.

Books will do this to you, or at least they've done it to me. Did God design things, or at least me, so that a book plus time might equal an astonished imagination or some other delight in God's heart? So my second favorite quotation about reading comes from Annie Dillard, recalling her childhood in Pittsburgh:

I began reading books, reading books to delirium. I began by vanishing from the known world into the passive abyss of

1. Thomas Merton, *Thoughts in Solitude* (New York: Noonday, 1956), 62.

> reading ... A book of fiction was a bomb. It was a land mine you
> wanted to go off. You wanted it to blow your whole day.[2]

Indeed. *The Call of the Wild* blew my day, and *The Thread that Runs So True* blew my dream of being an astronaut. I wonder if God had this sort of bomb-effect in mind when fashioning things, thinking a big book like the Bible might be just the thing to thrill our hearts.

Okay, so I have read a lot, whole afternoons or days or scheduled bedtimes unexpectedly blown (and I wish this had happened even more often). *The Hobbit* I read in a single sitting. The wisdom of taking Friday as a day off from ministry, something I'd resisted for years, made good sense the beautiful morning I chose not to go to work, sat in a lawn chair outside, and read the first 400 pages of Mark Helprin's *Soldier of the Great War*, and polished it off that night. Maybe God's busy while I'm doing this, but I like to envision God peering over my shoulder, digging the story even more than I do.

People who hear me talk, or read things I've written, sometimes ask: when do you find so much time to read? Are you a speed-reader? Years ago, I did take a speed-reading course, and the only thing I learned was that I have no desire to speed read. I suspect I'm a slow reader. I fully embrace being a slow reader—perhaps akin to Tolkien's Ents, those wise treelike creatures in *The Lord of the Rings*, who speak Entish, "a lovely language, but it takes a very long time to say anything in it, because we do not say anything in it, unless it is worth taking a long time to say, and to listen to."[3]

I've always read slowly, and I've always seemed to adore the books nobody else seems to like. I could claim this as the virtue of hospitality: we are supposed to welcome and love the people (and books) nobody else wants, right? But with reading it's a problem: a friend giddily presses a book he just finished into my hands, and weeks later I try to find some polite words for his book that put me to sleep. Or someone asks for a recommendation, I make one, and get a chilly remark the next time we meet. My self-assessment on this oscillates between a cocky elitism (I must be a more clever reader, not settling for best-selling bunk), and my default self-perception that I am just some misplaced alien on the wrong planet. The advantage (beyond feeling quirkily odd or special) is that I don't wind up with unreturned loaner books out there, and the spines of my

2. Annie Dillard, *An American Childhood* (New York: Harper Perennial, 1987), 80, 83.

3. J. R. R. Tolkien, *The Two Towers* (New York: Ballantine, 1954), 80.

well-cared-for books don't get broken. I have a proclivity for these books Mark Helprin described as "hard to read, that could devastate and remake one's soul, and that, when they were finished, had a kick like a mule."[4]

If I have read a lot, it is because I have never needed as much sleep as everybody else, and also because I am disciplined. At some point early in adult life, I made a compact with myself not to go to sleep without having read a bare minimum of at least fifty pages of something that day. I took some pride in this until I heard Pat Conroy's boast that he has read at least two hundred pages per day since his freshman year in high school. But fifty isn't bad. Do that 365 days a year, year after year, and you cover a lot of ground.

Small Sips and Long Swallows

I've also read frequently during the day—perhaps like President Kennedy, or Stephen King. In her conversions with Arthur Schlesinger, recorded just months after JFK's assassinations, Jacqueline Kennedy described her husband's reading habits, maintained during campaigns, hospitalizations, and the presidency:

> He read in the strangest way . . . He'd read walking, he'd read at the table, at meals, he'd read after dinner, he'd read in the bathtub, he'd read—prop open a book on his desk—on his bureau—while he was doing his tie . . . He'd open some book I'd be reading, you know, just devour it. He really read all the times you don't think you have time to read.[5]

And King, writer of such scary stuff as *Carrie* and *The Shining*, echoed my habits precisely:

> I take a book with me everywhere I go, and find there are all sorts of opportunities to dip in. The trick is to teach yourself to read in small sips as well as in long swallows. Waiting rooms were made for books. But so are theater lobbies, long boring checkout lines, and everyone's favorite, the john. You can even read while you're driving, thanks to the audiobook revolution.[6]

4. Mark Helprin, *Winter's Tale* (New York: Pocket, 1983), 211.

5. Jacequline Kennedy, *Historic Conversations on Life with John F. Kennedy: Interviews with Arthur M. Schlesinger, Jr., 1964* (New York: Hyperion, 2011), 40–41.

6. Stephen King, *On Writing: A Memoir of the Craft* (New York: Pocket, 2000), 142.

I can admit to some ambivalence about the audiobook, though. When I'm glad I listened, I'm frustrated, wishing I'd bought the book so I could circle and underline, and if I don't enjoy listening, I've wasted time and money: lose, lose.

A skilled narrator certainly can make wooden words spring to life. I shall never forget the time Lisa and I, facing a long drive, decided to listen to Rick Bragg read his *All Over But the Shoutin'*, with its profoundly sad stories, both public and personal. We were both reduced to tears we would not have shared reading privately, or perhaps reading at all. Over the centuries, if you think about it, the Bible has functioned more as an audiobook: a majority of folks, those who couldn't read or own books, have *heard* this book being read *to* them, sitting in a sanctuary or smaller gatherings.

And with an audio book, I can't flip back! In its infancy, Christianity had scrolls and parchment—but they were unwieldy. Little wonder Christians were the first people in the world to begin making the codex: a stack of individual pages, stitched together like a book—and why? They were eager to flip through from one passage to another. This urge to flip around is part of my reluctance to embrace the newfangled reading technologies, the Kindle and its competitors: I can't flip, check back quickly, thumb forward to the map insert, check the index to see if Dostoevsky is mentioned often. God favors flipping back. If we know God best in retrospect, then memory is just this, thumbing back to some flash of realization we'd missed the first time through.

Isn't this interesting? In our faith's earliest days, illiteracy was high, but the culture was still bookish. Christianity hinged entirely on books being read, at least out loud. I recall falling into a hush when I learned that in antiquity reading was always oral, that even when alone people read out loud; Augustine reported his surprise on seeing Ambrose reading silently.[7] Over 99 percent of my reading has been silent, the only exceptions being when my children were young and we read *Goodnight, Moon*; *The Lion, Witch and the Wardrobe*; *The Giving Tree*, and a shelf full of other favorites. I wish I had continued to read out loud—to hear words, to share words, and not just with the children. Eudora Welty wrote of a couple who, as they grew older, read to one another: it was "the breath of life flowing between them, and the words of the moment riding on it that held them in delight. Between some two people every word is beautiful."[8]

7. *Confessions* 6.3.3.
8. Eudora Welty, *The Optimist's Daughter* (New York: Vintage, 1968), 140.

Knowledge is Good

So, almost always in total silence, and generally alone, I have read fiction, non-fiction, biography, history, multiple histories and biographies of the same subject, science, economics, art history, travelogues, psychology, economics, and of course boatloads of theology, sports books, political and social commentary—you name it, I've read it. It's great fun, but I do lean toward the counsel that we should always sift through our motivations. Why am I not merely an avid reader, but also a driven, compulsive reader? Is there some sinister underbelly to this obsession, some desperately sought security in all this accumulated knowing? The apostle Paul warned about being "puffed up" with knowledge (1 Cor 8:1).

When it comes to writing there *is* such a thing: Thomas Merton spoke of his earliest publishing ventures, and acknowledged that

> My chief concern was to see myself in print. It was as if I could not be quite satisfied that I was real until I could feed my ambition with these trivial glories, and my ancient selfishness was now matured and concentrated in this desire to see myself externalized in a public and printed and official self which I could admire at my ease. This was what I really believed in: reputation, success. I wanted to live in the eyes and the mouths and the minds of men . . . But when my mind was absorbed in all that, how could I lead a supernatural life, the life to which I was called? How could I love God, when everything I did was done not for Him but for myself, and not trusting in His aid, but relying on my own wisdom and talents?[9]

Do I read so much to prop up my sense of being somebody?

And yet, knowing things is good. If I learn about something that transpired in Sicily in the fourteenth century, that fact is something God has known for centuries. If I learn about the echolocation of bats, I know a little about something God knows more thoroughly than Richard Dawkins (an avowed atheist!) who just explained it to me. If I am at a party and someone asks the parlor question, "With what famous person in history would you like to have dinner?" I might answer Winston Churchill or Abraham Lincoln or Eleanor of Aquitaine or Cicero—and I feel like I'd have a head start because of the terrific biographies I've read about them. Ponder the fact that God knows their secrets that eluded their biographers, and even their closest friends. If I wish Christians would take to the streets

9. Thomas Merton, *The Seven Storey Mountain* (New York: Harcourt Brace Jovanovich, 1948), 236.

and march to change the world once more, I know I'd be there since I've felt the courage, peril, and exhilaration from the riveting narratives of the civil rights movement I've digested.

Whatever was remembered or learned will be buried with me—unless we carry our learning into eternity with us. Will even a few of my books line my grandchildren's little antique shelves for decoration purposes? Will the rest be recycled and then be resurrected as . . . well, what happens to recycled paper? I'll have to order a book and read up on that. "Time like an ever rolling stream bears all its"—sons? books? away. Memory and books vanish, either into nothingness, or more likely into the vast expanse that is the mind of God, stored up with tender love, healed, rectified, reconciled. To dust my books shall return, like my body—and I wonder if the hope of resurrection might apply here. Nothing is finally lost, all is redeemed, the scattered universe regathered into the eternal, heavenly sanctuary of praise of God, every created mass and subatomic particle finding its place extolling the wonder of our Lord, like the perfect library containing all books written or even dreamed of being written ever, all read, digested, and appreciated.

Inevitable Plot Twists

Clearly, reading elicits humility, wonder, crushing disappointment, and yet an unsquelchable hope. Some things we never quite figure out, or get right. I am fond of the fact that Tolkien never felt happy with *The Lord of the Rings*, kept correcting, not releasing it to the publisher for many years. As a young man, Karl Barth started writing a book called *Church Dogmatics*, and kept at it for thirty-five years, and then he died, not done trying to say something true about God, the mess we're in, and the hope that is ours. I'm not done reading Barth, and I'm nowhere near done with my wish list of books, which lengthens as my remaining days shorten. Isn't it humbling, how much even the most avid reader has not read? I'm counting on eternal life to allow me borrowing privileges at the ancient library of Alexandria, which surely will be preserved there, and that I'll miraculously be granted facility in cuneiform, Mandarin, Dutch, and even olde English, which has always eluded me. Surely I'll have plenty of time to catch up on books I've not gotten around to. And I'll understand more, and make connections, and increasingly grasp the glory of God. Do the angels and saints glorify God by merely singing or gazing? Do they read? Are they the ones who have finally learned to read?

This business of learning how to read: I'd suppose my first books were about Jack and Jill, or Spot, or Christopher Columbus or some such character. Mrs. Brown patiently pointed to letters and taught phonics and quizzed us on vocabulary. At some point, you're in: I can read! But we're always learning how to read.

Certainly when it comes to scripture this is the case. One of the humbling but giddy delights of preaching is dusting off some terribly familiar passage, poking around for something to say, only to notice a word or turn of phrase or implication that had always been there, but you'd just never noticed it before. I believe this to be some droll whimsy in God's plan—that the Bible is so richly multifaceted so as to compel me and all God's people to keep coming back, to press further into the dark cave to dig up some new jewels. It's humbling: I have a PhD in Bible, multiple thick commentaries on every book of the Bible (crammed with my underlinings and marginalia), facility in Hebrew and Greek, and yet every week there's something as plain as the nose on my face I flat out flew past in twenty-seven prior readings.

This unexpectedness is of course the thrill in reading. But then we learn to value what is not at all unexpected, what you noticed fully before, and it was so lovely you revel in it again, and again, like your favorite dish, or chocolate cake, sunset at the shore, your grandmother's smile, or that symphony or romantic pop favorite. My children, like all children, exhibited an intense glee in repetition. Night after night we turned the pages to *Goodnight, Moon*, spotting the mouse in the window sill, the timbre of voice ever softer, night after night. Comfort in the familiarity, the simple mirth of routine: we know what's coming, and thank God for such loveliness and the bonds of sleepiness.

There is another sort of cunning the good writers employ that can make you shiver, grin, moan—and intuit the kind of thing God is about. It might be a whodunit, or any story with an unfolding, yet to be resolved plot. You wonder how it will all turn out, you just have no idea, you have a few hunches—and then, Bam! It was the butler! And you sigh, slap your knee, and say "Wow, I didn't see that coming—but *of course* it was the butler!" Ever since Aristotle, writers have understood the virtue of the surprise ending that, once it's known, is no surprise at all; we didn't see it coming, but it couldn't have turned out any other way. In her beguiling novels about sordid dramas among Church of England folks, Susan Howatch repeatedly employs the technique of ending a major section with a knock at the door; whoever answers the door is as stunned as the reader, and everything makes sense, or the plot thickens.

Sometimes you see it coming—"it" being the climax, the resolution, the identification of the culprit, the heroic destiny fulfilled, and "it" still stuns and titillates. Sometimes when asked What is your favorite novel? (and it's only "sometimes"—how can a single book fill that bill?), I answer *A Prayer for Owen Meany*, a book that, page by page, left me sighing, prodded me to giggle out loud, moved me to tears, and of course, gave me the shivers. When it ended the way John Irving had for six hundred pages told me it would end, I was crushed, delirious, sad, joyful—and wished I could rewind and do it all over again.

My seminary professor, David Steinmetz, suggested that the narrative of salvation in many ways is like one of those mysteries, in which a sprawling story doesn't seem headed anywhere, characters displaying their flaws, events unfolding—but then the investigator, be it Sherlock Holmes, Miss Marple, or Inspector Dalgleish, steps in at the end and retells the whole story, not a new story or a subplot, but the real story you've been witnessing all along, but now it all makes sense. The Bible, similarly, has a long plot that often is going no place, with bad behavior, heroic moments, puzzlement over how it will all turn out—but then we are made privy to the ending, and the narrative really does hang together, as does all of human history, and even my own life. This notion oddly helps me see not only the Bible as a whole entity, but also my life as perhaps not as random as it feels. Yes, I'm terribly confused just now, and tomorrow will be bleak no matter how hard I try. But the Savior will step in, ultimately, redeem it all and make sense of yesterday's muddle.

Premature Assignments

Part of the muddle that is our life in reading is not merely that we miss reading great books, but we read them at the wrong phase of life. *A Prayer for Owen Meany* resonated deeply in me when I read it—but would it have done as lovely a work in me had I read it twenty years later? The crassest mis-timing of the reading of the canon of great books is that schoolteachers assign them. The very act of compelling a fifteen-year-old to read a book sinks any chance of said book speaking deeply. It's homework, it's drudgery, it's not something I chose, so it's boring. Rifle through the *Cliff's Notes* and be done with it.

More problematical is that large, profound books require readers who've experienced large, profound lives; so a teen with a thin, sheltered life thus far won't have the proper mental and spiritual grid needed for understanding. If you'd asked me about *Silas Marner* when I was in tenth grade, I would have replied with a single word: "miser." The guy was a miser, and I hurried through his story to be able to supply the word "miser" on a quiz.

But after getting a few years under my belt, having lost and gained much, and veering more often than I'd care to admit into a crusty, dark, crotchety mode of merely existing for my work and its trifling payments, I reread *Silas Marner* (or really read it for the first time). I found myself flummoxed, and so very happy, wondering how I'd missed this little gem. This wretched miser suffered the theft of his gold. But on returning home one evening, he found a sleeping child, a wonder.

> He had a dreamy feeling that this child was somehow a message come to him from a far-off life . . . We older human beings feel a certain awe in the presence of a little child, such as we feel before some quiet majesty or beauty in earth or sky.[10]

Marner named her Eppie. He took the little girl on his lap, "trembling with an emotion mysterious to himself, at something unknown dawning on his life. He could only have said that the child was come instead of the gold— that the gold had turned into this child." This child, whom he named Eppie, loved sunshine, sounds, and every other thing in God's world. Her joy awakened joy in him.

For most children, including those assigned *Silas Marner* in school, Eppies are everywhere. But an aging man craves the surprise of just one. Of course, I see the gift of the child Jesus as just such an Eppie-wonderment—that is, if we bend down in the dark and feel our way for what we've lost and will never regain, and then let the Christ child lure us out into the sunshine to discover that some power really is presiding over life.

Back to books assigned prematurely: I first hustled through the *Iliad* and the *Odyssey* in ninth grade. If recollection serves, I was mildly drawn to the fighting: what adolescent male couldn't fixate on Hector and Achilles engaged in mortal combat?

But now that I'm three times as old as I was when I first read the *Iliad*, I realize that the power of Homer wasn't the fighting, but the abyss of emotion in those who loved the fighters. Rereading in my late forties, I

10. George Eliot, *Silas Marner* (New York: Bantam Classic, 1981), 119, 124.

shuddered and blinked back tears when I came upon the gripping, viscerally devastating scene in which Andromache learns of Hector's death:

> My heart is in my throat, my knees are like ice . . .
> O God, I'm afraid Achilles has cut off my brave Hector . . .
> And has put an end to my husband's
> Cruel courage . . .
> With these words on her lips Andromache
> Ran outdoors like a madwoman, heart racing . . .
> She reached the tower, pushed through the crowd,
> And looking out from the wall saw her husband
> As the horses dragged him disdainfully . . .
> Black night swept over her eyes.
> She reeled backward, gasping, and her veil
> And glittering headbands flew off . . .
> "Hector, you and I have come to the grief
> We were both born for . . .
> And now you are going to Hades' dark world,
> Underground, leaving me in sorrow,
> A widow in the halls, with an infant,
> The son you and I bore but cannot bless."[11]

When the book club of biblical writers, Matthew, Paul, Isaiah, Luke, Moses, David, Peter, and John meet, do they turn green with envy over the depth of insight conveyed by Homer? David's poignant lament over the demise of Saul is memorable:

> Thy glory, O Israel, is slain . . .
> How the mighty have fallen . . .
> Saul and Jonathan, beloved and lovely!
> In life and in death they were not divided;
> they were swifter than eagles, stronger than lions.
> Ye daughters of Israel, weep over Saul (2 Sam 1:19, 23, 24).

But Homer's dramatic depiction of Andromache takes the prize, hands down.

Or consider the victor, Achilles, ambivalent about his destiny, and how his vocation is intertwined with his mother's emotions.

> My mother Thetis, a moving silver grace,
> Tells me two fates sweep me on to my death.
> If I stay here and fight, I'll never return home,
> But my glory will be undying forever.

11. Homer, *Iliad*, trans. Stanley Lombardo (Indianapolis: Hackett, 1997), 437f.

> If I return home to my dear fatherland
> My glory is lost but my life will be long.[12]

Has Mary in heaven ever read these words (or might she just possibly have overheard them in her own lifetime?) and thought of her son's dilemma at Golgotha?

Lingering with this oddball (yet hopefully not impertinent) possibility of the biblical writers wondering if they might have done better: when I try to talk about, or live into personal adventures like forgiveness or generosity, as fond as I am of the scriptures, I find myself thumbing through some favored moments in Marilynne Robinson's *Gilead*. Admittedly, *Gilead* is only my second favorite of her books (*Housekeeping* gets that vote).

Her depictions of the way a man tells about his grandfather, who "never kept anything that was worth giving away, or let us keep it, either, so my mother said. He would take laundry right off the line. She said he was worse than any thief, worse than a house fire . . . I believe he was a saint of some kind." This reckless giving away of tools, food, and even the blankets off the bed in winter is labeled "an earned innocence," "a holy poverty," as he made life hard for his family, but they loved him, realizing he was "just afire with old certainties."[13]

And then her closing scene, the unforgettable moment of simultaneous parting and reconciliation between old Boughton and his son, a forgiveness that even knows how to be "grateful for all my old bitterness of heart"? Well—I can't begin to summarize it. You just have to read the book for yourself. I would bet that book club of the biblical writers are similarly gratified, when an author notices something embedded in the biblical phenomena, and then finds a way to rearticulate it so we might see, and then be able not only to speak freshly and more deeply about forgiveness and generosity, but actually forgive and give away the clothes off our own lines.

Read For Yourself

I skipped over my desperate plea just now: "You just have to read the book for yourself." Indeed. I've acknowledged I've never been a trusted recommender, but I do have my favorites, many of which I've touched upon already. Graham Greene's *End of the Affair* (but also *The Heart of the*

12. Ibid., 171.

13. Marilynne Robinson, *Gilead* (New York: Farrar, Straus and Giroux, 2004), 31.

Matter), George Eliot's *Adam Bede* (which I like more than her more wide-ly acclaimed *Middlemarch*), Barbara Kingsolver's *Poisonwood Bible* (which should be required reading for any religious person eager to spread their beliefs), Carlos Zaphon's *Shadow of the Wind* (a book about lots of books!). A smidgeon embarrassed to admit this, I've even indulged in genres alien to my own tastes, with much delight: time travel (Jack Finegan's charming *Time and Again*), science fiction (I think Mary Doria Russell's *The Sparrow* is the only sci-fi novel I've ever read, and I thank God for it)—and even vampires (Elisabeth Kostova's *The Historian*, which I flat out could not put down and lost much sleep because of it).

I've mentioned John Irving's *A Prayer for Owen Meany*. My now flagging love affair with Irving began one night when I watched the film version of *The World According to Garp* on television. Oh my. I nabbed the paperback and devoured it in two or three sittings, and settled on the an-swer to the parlor game question, Which is better, the movie or the book? With *Garp* my reply is Both. Then I moved on to *Owen Meany*, then to *Cider House Rules*, which was jarringly wonderful. I waited eagerly for his next gem.

And I kept waiting. Disappointment grew as successive novels ap-peared from Irving's hand. Starting with his awful *Son of the Circus*, I found his writing to be less intriguing emotionally, too much as if he was putting his writing craft on display, and frankly trashy. I'm no prude, and *Owen Meany*, *Garp,* and *Cider House* have plenty of edgy sex and crude-ness. But I was missing the nobility, the hope, the profound feelings that make life and reading worth bothering about.

I was fortunate enough to have lunch with Frederick Buechner once when he was in town giving a lecture. Somehow the conversation drifted to Irving, and Buechner told me Irving was his neighbor up in Vermont. I guess great authors really do enjoy mundane realities like neighbors as we all do. He agreed with me that Irving's work had been in considerable decline—and said he paid Irving a visit to talk about it. Buechner rather wonderfully reported to me that he said, "John, when you wrote *A Prayer for Owen Meany*, the world got a little bit better. If you have that kind of gift, you can't waste it." A book making the world a bit better! One writer urging another to be his best self. Oh my.

Why do we prefer one book to another? Is it like tasting wine, or digging bacon cheeseburgers over a tofu wrap? Sometimes a great writer rises to a great subject; I think of William Manchester's witty and eloquent volumes on the life of Winston Churchill (and I've never quite forgiven

Manchester for dying before finishing the third volume). So perhaps it is not merely that we depend upon the great writer to tell us about great subjects; it probably is the case that great subjects, grand lives or riveting happenings or chains of events do not need great writing so much as they create great writers. Perhaps some symbiosis happens: great writer encounters great subject, and the alchemy is sizzling.

On my shelf are a few dozen books about St. Francis (including my own contribution to the pile, *Conversations with St. Francis*), ranging from the scholarly to the popular, the soundly-reasoned to the ridiculous. My favorite will forever be G. K. Chesterton, not because he was a more incisive reader of medieval texts, or because he knew the hermitages, caves and chiesas of Umbria, Tuscany and the Rieti valley better than the others, but because of his felicity of expression. Francis "seemed to have liked everybody, but especially those whom everybody disliked him for liking." "The man who knows he cannot pay his debt . . . will be always throwing things away into a bottomless pit of unfathomable thanks." And it is not only that Chesterton could coin memorable phrases; that very ability enabled him to understand what others might miss, like the meaning of Francis's austerity: "His asceticism was in one sense the height of optimism. He demanded a great deal of human nature not because he despised it but because he trusted it."[14]

The key is Chesterton's charming style. He wrote with a cheeky, pithy cleverness not only spoke articulately about Francis, but that was itself, as a style, entirely fitting to the puckish, playful manner of life that was the secret of Francis's appeal. So writing style rose up to give flawless expression to the one written about. This happens more rarely than we realize— and perhaps exposes a secret to the rambling, earthy, prosaic, and profane stories, songs, letters, and sagas that make up our Bible. Far from apologizing for such a vehicle to express a more sublime God, the scriptures invite us to know a God who is and can only be portrayed in wickedly secular tales of dysfunctional families, missives dashed off in a panic, angry street preachers railing against religious folks, and the haunting biography of someone who looked as ungodlike as possible while saving every last one of us.

So, one of Chesterton's unforgettable insights is that "it is very enlightening to realize that Christ was like St. Francis." Too often we reverse that simile, thinking the mimicry comes only from our side. But it truly

14. G. K. Chesterton, *St. Francis of Assisi* (Garden City, NY: Image, 1957), 47, 80, 104, 117.

is helpful to notice that Christ was very much like Francis, a real person, an unordained, stylish guy with friends, and from troubled parents. God is known via families at odds with one another, deception and mayhem, scoundrels and pretenders, a small nation that barely survived and then didn't, a temple reduced to rubble, a hairy locust-eating shouter, a teacher nobody understood except social outcasts and the morally bankrupt, and a movement that struggled for decades to get a little traction, and then became big, and staid, and too often mean. Somehow the real God is remembered truly through all these things, and in no other way.

Simply to Notice

Perhaps because I was a science junkie as a kid, I've read a good bit of popular science, and don't mind all the skepticism and downright hostility toward God among the writers I adore: Richard Dawkins, Stephen Jay Gould, and the amazing Stephen Hawking. He got a lot of press for his conclusion (in *The Grand Design*) that God is not necessary, that we can explain all that is without resorting to God. Quite a few anxious believers asked me to counter and to debunk, but it occurred to me that God does not mind Stephen Hawking, and may actually be pleased to be conceived of as unnecessary. God would not compel anyone to believe. The possibility of God not being, or at least not being in one's thinking and desiring, is required for believers to believe. Love doesn't force, or demand assent. Love is vulnerable. Love is always ready to be pushed off to the side.

So I think any time a smart person shares what they know, or think they know, God is pleased. What God wants us to do, above all, is to pay attention—which is why one of my top five recommended books will forever be Annie Dillard's *Pilgrim at Tinker Creek*. She has taken the time to watch hummingbirds, loons and glaciers, and then testified that we live in a marvelous world, a profligate symphony of life, the steady omnipresence of death, the ineluctable triumph of beauty and hope.

Her consistent, alluring counsel? After watching a mockingbird swooping downward repeatedly over several minutes, she compares his free fall to "the old philosophical conundrum about the tree that falls in the forest. The answer must be, I think, that beauty and grace are performed whether or not we will or sense them. The least we can do is try to be there." Later she adds, "I cannot cause light; the most I can do is try to put myself in the path of its beam."[15] Ours is simply to notice. I want to

15. Annie Dillard, *Pilgrim at Tinker Creek* (New York: HarperCollins, 1974), 8, 33.

add "and to praise God," but I wonder: isn't it the case that God is actually praised when anyone's jaw drops when a flower or cloud or a horse standing out in a field is noticed, and admired, or analyzed by a scientist, even if God is not explicitly named by the one doing the noticing and studying?

Isn't biography the noticing of human life? I cannot be sure why I've read so many biographies. It is not a self-improvement program. A human life is simply interesting; and frankly, some are more interesting than others. History turns on a few lives—and the Bible is by and large biography, with a theological slant. So I see on my shelves more than one biography each of Christopher Columbus, Dorothy Day, John Kennedy, Franklin Roosevelt, Teddy Roosevelt, Thomas Jefferson, Michelangelo, Caravaggio, Thérèse of Lisieux, Luther, Eleanor of Aquitaine, Augustine, Chrysostom, Martin Luther King, Gandhi, Churchill, LBJ. I've tried to write a bit of biography myself, and I think the best compliment of my writing I've ever received came from David Steinmetz, the great Reformation scholar and my teacher, who said this about my little digest of the lives of various luminaries throughout Christian history, *Servants, Misfits, and Martyrs: Saints and their Stories*: "I gave it to my mother, knowing she would like it and then know about the people I've been writing about all these years."

David, when he taught me in seminary and graduate school, introduced me to a host of books by and about Augustine, Luther, Aquinas, Lady Julian, and Calvin. "Introduced" is a gentle word for the way professors force reading upon their students—and what a great gift that can be. On a whim in college, I registered for a course called "Existentialism," not really certain what that might be. The professor assigned me a paper on Kierkegaard; I plunged in, and didn't surface for air for a few months, or years actually. Now I thumb through books I read in college and seminary, by Kierkegaard and countless others, and I get a little crinkly grin when I see all the underlinings, circlings, scribbles in the margins, arrows, exclamation points, like the indentations your molars might make on a hunk of meat or loaf of bread if you had been starved for some time.

Since I am certain I did not pause in those college and graduate school days to thank God for the books, those who wrote them or the instructors who assigned them, I must do so now. What was my hunger that led to such greedy devouring? Learning to read Bible in Hebrew and Greek was no drudgery, but heady fun. I like the way the original languages don't make you a smarter reader so much as they simply force you to slow down and ask careful questions about a word or phrase. Part of me was striving to establish my intellectual worth. I also saw and perhaps understood myself for the very first time when I read of Luther's anxiety-riddled darkness, Augustine and some pals stealing pears, and even the impatient rabble-rousing of Dorothy Day, who was still alive when I began to examine her life, which turned into an examination of my own.

Bookstores and Book Clubs

How do we find and pick which books to read among such a laughably massive variety? We all have other readers we trust. I watch for footnotes, where authors either try to buttress their authority or actually shuttle you off to your next great read. With the Internet we can browse an endless selection of books, although I still prefer the bookstore and library, where the hunting is tactile: you bend over, sit on the floor, reach up high, your feet ache after a while. Another blown afternoon.

I was never in a book club (and would have scoffed at the notion) until well into my fifties. The first I didn't want to join, but my unadulterated admiration for the man who invited me left me no option. We have read some pretty heady fiction. At least half the guys in this group (not religious guys, and a couple of them can be outright hostile to matters of faith) are more brilliant assessors of literature than I thought might populate the literature departments of Harvard and Stanford.

The most delightful and humbling moment with this group came when we had read John Banville's dense and fascinating *The Infinities*, a book I'd worked hard on and felt I had a decent grasp upon. Then the host started thumbing through the novel, would pick a passage he had marked, and ask, "Now what does this sentence remind you of?" The other excessively brilliant ones in the group would say "Oh, yes, that scene in *Ulysses*," or "An obvious allusion to *The Sound and the Fury*," or "The language mimics Bronte." The rest of us in the group slinked down into our chairs, but felt honored to be members (or observers and admirers) of such a group.

Then a second club, soon thereafter: my neighbor and I discovered we both loved history, and over a bourbon one afternoon thought up the idea of finding some like-minded men who would read history (primarily military!) and even try to get authors and experts to meet with us. This was a resounding success.

The idea of having the writer present: as a reader, I can easily become a gushing groupie when I get to meet a great author—although when I find myself in the presence of some luminary I've fawned over for years, I get tongue-tied. I've shaken hands with John Irving and Walter Cronkite (on tour touting his autobiography)—and spent thirty awkward minutes with Jimmy and Rosalynn Carter. I got to sit next to Elie Wiesel at an elegant luncheon. What to say? "Hey, I really enjoyed *Night*"?

But I can report two successes: I made Shelby Foote (the darling of Civil War buffs) laugh out loud, and I think I brought a tear to Pat Conroy's eyes. Foote was in Charlotte giving a talk, and Lisa arranged for me to meet him at a reception in someone's home. He was sitting alone on the couch, so I screwed up my courage and plopped down next to him. Out of the blue I found myself telling him about the time I showed up at the park ranger's office in Guinea Station, Virginia (in the house where Stonewall Jackson died), which serves two battlefields, Chancellorsville and Spotsylvania Courthouse. As dusk was drawing near, I asked the ranger on duty, "If I only have time to visit one battle site, which should I pick?" He didn't blink, and answered assuredly, "Chancellorsville, of course. We won that one." And Shelby Foote laughed—a long, deep, hearty laugh—and slapped me on my knee. I envy myself that moment when I think of it.

Then Lisa made similar arrangements when Pat Conroy was in town. We were told he would happily autograph books—so we purchased crisp hardbacks of *The Great Santini*, *The Lords of Discipline*, and *The Prince of Tides*. When I handed him *The Lords of Discipline*, I opened the book to the very last page, not the frontispiece, and asked if he wouldn't mind signing there. He smiled immediately, paused, and looked visibly moved—and if you're wondering why, read the last page of the book for yourself. I think I envy him that moment, for the prospect of writing something, and then realizing somebody really understood the best, deepest aspect of what you've written, must be immensely rewarding.

Reading and Writing

So now the subject has been fully broached: I'm a reader who not only admired writers but feigned to become one. I've seen this in my life as a minister. There are quite a few people (never enough!) who admire the clergy, who are attentive to the preacher, who appreciate the pastoral visitor. But once in a while, some tipping point is passed, and a woman or a man shifts from admiring what I do to actually wanting to *do* what I do.

I do not remember when I stepped over from loving books, and then harboring much adulation for writers, into the crazed ambition actually to be a writer. Of course, I never bothered with the fantasy that I might write like the great ones. But I did want my name on the spine of a book—whether it was because I had something important to say somebody needed to read, or because I had something important I just wanted to say, or even because I thought I could cement my worth by being a permanent entry in a library catalog.

I wrote a typically dull dissertation to complete my PhD, designed to impress a tiny band of scholars who might pick it up. I tried my hand at adult Sunday School literature, but that was frustrating. I composed a few articles to submit to journals and got summarily rejected. I then cobbled together a few partial manuscripts, with no clarity of purpose, no sense of the audience, piling up too many complicated thoughts. Finally I actually completed a rough draft of a book, and then another book; thankfully, neither saw the light of day. They were, I think, a lot like the earnest young lover who jabbers away, well-intended but gangly, a jumble of confused thoughts. In retrospect I can see quite clearly that I wanted to be a writer far more than I actually had something to say, again in the way a young lover simply wants to be a lover more than he is prepared actually to love another real human being meaningfully.

Years slipped by; rejection notices began to pile up—or worse, often there was simply no notice of any kind. Someone gave me one of those books that has collected the early rejection notices of writers who eventually became famous. Not encouraging: were we to gather the rejection notices of writers who remained forever rejected, we could fill many sizable rooms, not just this cute book. I thought about the biblical "writers," and wondered how many false starts and unpublished treasures came from their minds, mouths and pens. Did Paul try to say something to the Corinthians, but then wad it up in exasperation? Did Jeremiah's best sermon fail to be recorded? Was one of Jesus's disciples, maybe Nathaniel or Andrew, working on a gospel that was never finished because of a hasty departure in the face of persecution, or simply an early death from infection?

I tried to lighten up. I tried to write about things I actually cared about. I struggled to find my voice—and a publisher. At long last, I latched on to an old idea I'd harbored for a long time, and it became my first book, *Yours Are the Hands of Christ*. I shall never forget when the first copy arrived; if entering the gates of heaven is better than this I will be surprised. I brought it home to show Lisa, who had cheered for me throughout this long process, and had even dared to suggest I had immense worth even if I never got anything published. She thumbed through, excitedly—and then

I asked her to read the dedication page, which thanked various friends for helping me write about Jesus' hands, and then named her,

> my wife, who is a voracious reader of mysteries and of all the stuff I put out. This book is dedicated to her. Her own hands are remarkable. With them she expresses the ineffable through liturgical dance. With them she frames and hammers nails in Habitat houses. With them she does a thousand little things that make our house a home and our community a better place.

Smooth. I discovered the perfect gift to give my wonderful in-laws on their fiftieth anniversary: a book on the Holy Spirit dedicated to them. And it was fun to hand my book on the creed, dedicated to my great friends Jason Byassee and Craig Kocher, to Craig just minutes before he led the congregation at Duke Chapel in that creed at a service where I was the guest preacher. Big smiles across the chancel.

Writing as Prayer

Marilynne Robinson was probably speaking for herself (and unintentionally for me) when she conceived of a dying old man writing things he wanted his grandson to read later: "For me writing has always felt like praying . . . You feel that you are with someone. I feel I am with you now, whatever that can mean."[16] I shall not ramble on here about writing—although for me it is like praying in that I hope that whenever I wind up before God's judgment seat, I can open up my little backpack of books, and splay them out on the floor, and God will be pleased. Perhaps not awed, but at least honored.

Once in a while the prayer that is writing surprisingly is answered. A few times someone has been kind enough to say that one of my books, or something else I wrote, really mattered. I think I know of two lives I saved. One evening when I was not home, our telephone rang. My son, sixteen at the time, answered. A man on the other end explained he was thinking about taking his life. Someone had given him one of my books; I do not know which one. He read something that lit a faint candle in his darkness—so in desperation he hunted down my number and called. Noah got the gentleman's number, we connected later that night, and walked through a few tough weeks together—even though he was in Wisconsin and I in North Carolina.

16. Marilynne Robinson, *Gilead* (New York: Farrar, Straus, and Giroux, 2004), 19.

Struck from Behind

Then a few years back I travelled to another city to give a talk. A woman who appeared to be in her early twenties ran up to me and hugged me for an almost uncomfortable period of time. I scrambled to try to recall who she might be. Tearfully but almost giggling, she explained that I had baptized her when she was a few weeks old. When she was fifteen, she sunk into a morbid depression, could not get herself out of bed, and contemplated suicide. Her parents tried psychiatrists, pills, prayer chains, but nothing availed.

Cleaning out a drawer, they stumbled upon a letter I had written—and I bet there are hundreds of such letters, jammed in cabinets, scrapbooks, or perhaps in a landfill somewhere. After I baptize a child, the parents get a letter I've written to the child, with encouragement to keep it and give it to the child once he or she is grown. Nothing brilliant, just a little message about the meaning of baptism, the grace of God, a simple "whatever happens you are always a beautiful child of God" sentiment. Same letter, generated by a secretary, written my first year in ministry, mailed over and over to people I assumed paid little attention, more a keepsake than anything else. Unbelievable as it seemed to me, one of those letters was kept by this young woman's parents, and retrieved in desperation. Even more miraculously, she read it, got out of bed and went to school, and kept going to school, then college, and now was engaged to be married.

A Little Pushcart Full

Paul wrote that the fruit of the Spirit is patience. Like most frenetic, type A personality Americans, I often bemoan my lack of patience (which thinly cloaks a perverse pridefulness, doesn't it?). I wonder if God has used the discipline of reading fifty pages daily, and writing things, even a single simple letter over and over and over, to weave some patience into my soul.

I'll wind up this reflection on reading by thinking once more about Karl Barth. How much time have I spent with this man? When I got out of seminary, feeling like I had years of reading ahead of me, I decided to embark on an intrepid journey through the thirteen thick volumes of Karl Barth's *Dogmatics*—more than six million words in 8 to 10 point font covering nearly 8,000 pages. I'd been familiar with Barth, of course. He wasn't your classic PhD academic theologian; he'd begun as a pastor in a little village—just like me!

I've always been fond of Barth's self-effacing assessment of his gargantuan production:

The angels laugh at old Karl. They laugh at him because he tried
to grasp the truth about God in a book of *Dogmatics*. They laugh
at the fact that a volume follows volume and each is thicker than
the previous one. As they laugh, they say to one another, "Look!
Here he comes now with his little pushcart full of volumes of the
Dogmatics!"[17]

Weighing the transient nature of even the greatest of books, he remarked
that

in heaven we shall know all that is necessary, and we shall not
have to write on paper or read any more. Indeed, I shall be able
to dump even the *Church Dogmatics*, over the growth of which
the angels have long been amazed, on some heavenly floor as a
pile of waste paper.[18]

Perhaps such will be the fate of my library, and certainly of the books I
have written (like this one), and those you have read.

So I decided to read Barth's 8,000 plus pages. I purchased my own
little pushcart of *Dogmatics* and began, with a goal of six pages per day.
Five years, even skipping a few days, and I would be done. I could not have
been more entranced, and I cannot conceive of a richer continuing education project for a young clergy person. Within months, I was graced by
two surprises. The first: I was told that the clergy in my area were to go on
retreat, so I went, not knowing the agenda dictated this would be a *silent*
retreat. Imagine: clergy, people who yack for a living, not being able to say
anything. I thought, naturally, "I'll read"—but the leader had advised us to
fast entirely from words, including those on a printed page. Not reading
would be harder than not talking.

Then the participants were subjected to personality tests: Myers-
Briggs, MMPI, Enneagram—and I harbor a lifelong cynicism about such
measurements, for their diagnosis can't pinpoint drivers who cut me off in
traffic, or voters who select boneheaded candidates, or people who frankly
aren't so nice to me. But I filled out the answer sheets, and then met the
next day with a counselor who wanted to talk about my spirituality. I know
church people think clergy are deeply pious, zealously prayerful, and unabashedly holy—but I knew myself to be pretty worldly, and utterly unable
to focus in prayer for more than about five seconds. I tried to read spiritual

17. Joseph L. Mangina, *Karl Barth: Theologian of Christian Witness* (Louisville:
Westminster, 2004), 25.

18. Eberhard Busch, *Karl Barth: His Life from Letters and Autobiographical Texts*,
trans. John Bowden (Philadelphia: Fortress, 1976), 489.

books, even the great devotional classics, but I found myself bored, or asleep within minutes. What is wrong with me? I heard about people seeing God in nature, in the trees and rivers—but when I go outside I think about playing football or getting some exercise. A sunset, to me, means it's time for dinner.

So I braced myself, expecting to be scolded for my ineptness in things of the spirit. Instead, this woman began as if she'd been privileged to live in my head for years: "So, let me guess: you don't really get off on a walk in the woods, and you find devotional literature dull." Was that in the MMPI? "Let me also guess a couple of other things: you feel closest to God when, number 1, you are singing hymns with the congregation, and number 2, you are reading dense, difficult theology." I wanted to jump up and hug this stranger who knew me better than I'd known myself. Yes, yes, yes. Evidently, I am the type of person who is wired to dig complex reading. I'd been trying to force myself to put Barth down and do some praying or reflecting on the *Upper Room*—when in fact, Barth and his tribe were God's great gift to draw me closer to God's own heart and mind.

I returned home and read Barth with a more relaxed abandon, and that leads me to the second debt I owe to his *Dogmatics*. Not reared to think well theologically, and having been so focused on historical matters and philosophical issues during my seminary and PhD years, I did not have a robust sense of what Jesus was about, or even what the enterprise of theology was about. God I could speak of; but Jesus, beyond being a first century, rather astonishing person who pointed accurately to God and embodied an exemplary holiness, had no higher role to play. Consequently, I would have fallen into the category of many mainline pastors and Christians, those who see religion as being basically about us, our faith, our spirituality, our good works for God, and our transcendent link is to an invisible, ineffable, faceless deity.

Barth invited me onto his stunning pilgrimage of neo-orthodoxy. His impact on me was precisely the impact he was determined to have on the entire Protestant world: declaring that theology is about God, not us; that it is not about our quest for God but God's pursuit of us; that the center of all thinking about God is Jesus, and that he is Lord, Savior, all those identities the creeds grappled to understand, a living, vital everything for the church and the world.

To think as highly as possible of Jesus, to see him as the very face of God, the literal embodiment of the divine heart, much loved within the Trinitarian life and being the way for me to be drawn into that life: in retrospect I would say such thinking would be self-evident for an ordained person, but of course it is not at all. For me, it was this reading of Barth that awakened the soul of theology in me, and built a reliable scaffold on which I constructed a ministry—and simultaneously was ushered into the presence of God through the simple act of reading day by day.

Epilogue

NOW THAT WE HAVE come to the end—which isn't the end at all, since I'm still typing—I think of a lovely thought I discovered in Marilynne Robinson's terrific novel, *Housekeeping*:

> Every memory is turned over and over again, every word, however chance, written in the heart in the hope that memory will fulfill itself, and become flesh, and that the wanderers will find a way home, and the perished, whose lack we always feel, will step through the door finally and stroke our hair with dreaming, habitual fondness, not having meant to keep us waiting long.[1]

This idea of memory fulfilling itself, and becoming flesh: now we're talking. If I thought at all about God as a child or in my adolescence, I believe the only item that I conceived to be in God's zone of interest would be whether I get into heaven or not when I die. By my second year in seminary, my mind had been blown, as I discovered that the Bible and wise theologians imagined a far larger God, with grander plans than sitting in a booth dispensing tickets to eternal life. God quite understandably had a vision for the whole cosmos, settling for nothing less than the redemption of everything. How lovely and hopeful, how staggering, how fitting!

So heaven won't merely be a reunion of the people who got their tickets stamped. Memories will take on flesh, past will be caught up into present and future, and those I've loved and lost will be even more present than they were back then, and the sorrows will be healed, the wrong turns righted. We will have wandered long enough, and then we will be at home, the home we've tried to return to but found ourselves foiled, supplied with milk and cookies, churned ice cream, words of love and tenderness,

---

1. Marilynne Robinson, *Housekeeping* (New York: Picador, 1980), 195.

fractured relationships glued back together so the seams don't show, and no one of us ever feel small again.

How will I live until then? I will try not to repeat mistakes I recall making, although success will be no more than partial. I will turn and look back for the truth that does strike from behind. I will try to relax any anxious grip on the past, and do my darnedest to choose gratitude over regret. What I have had I will not give back, even the painful parts.

St. Augustine was the historic master of theological autobiography. At the end of his own life, he thought all he had worked for was on the verge of oblivion, his home and the crumbling Roman empire overrun by hordes of Vandals. Bedridden with a spiking fever, Augustine asked that Psalms be copied out in large letters and hung on his walls so he could read them—or rather, pray them. The Psalms have figured prominently in my story, and I hope in my waning moments I will read and pray these words to God that have become for us the Word of God. They are full of memory and gratitude, remorse and forgiveness, boldness and hope, and finally the praise and glorification of God—and if they are full of all this, perhaps I will be also. If I remember correctly, this would be the recommended way to go, especially if some of those I've loved are there to send me off to God, and to those I've loved and lost.